What people are saying about
Who Are You and What Do You Want?

"If you sense uneasiness in your life and wonder if there is something better for you out there, you will love this book. The authors use thought-provoking questions and stories from remarkable people to lead and inspire you to make choices that will change your life to one of passion and fulfillment."

Rolf Benirschke, former San Diego Chargers kicker; author of *Alive and Kicking*

"This book is your road map to physical, spiritual, and emotional well-being. Finding out who you are and what makes life worth living isn't easy. It wasn't meant to be easy. It requires living in the truth, and by doing so you'll forge relationships, attain goals, and achieve real happiness and harmony. *Who Are You* will help keep you focused on the cup being half-full and keep you on track to be the best you can be in all aspects of work, love, and life."

Colin Cowie, author of *Colin Cowie Chic* and *Extraordinary Weddings!*

"Not only did my wife and I love the book, we've already ordered a copy for each of our children, ages 16 to 29, so that they can benefit from Ukleja's and Lorber's wisdom and the life lessons as they make important decisions about careers, families, and the direction they want their lives to progress."

Bob Eckert, chairman and CEO, Mattel, Inc.

"Authors Mick Ukleja and Robert Lorber show us that the real path to long-term success and happiness is to be truthful with ourselves and to find the best of ourselves now. The advice in this book is timeless, essential, life-changing—and a must-read."

Peter Economy, associate editor, *Leader to Leader*

"A remarkable new book that will surely alter the substance, value, and course of the reader's life—it offers a unique and individualized approach to achieving intermediate and long-term life goals."

Stephen Feldman, Ph.D., president, Astronauts
Memorial Foundation, Kennedy Space Center, and
author of *Smart Money*

"Mick and Bob have knocked one out of the park in this refreshing and inspiring must-read. This practical and user-friendly model not only helps you nail down what you really want out of life but also provides the road map and practical tools to help you get there. This is your personal game plan that you'll pass on to your kids!"

Pat Gillick, senior vice-president and general
manager, Philadelphia Phillies

"*Who Are You and What Do You Want?* is an excellent primer for people just starting out in life or for those who are ready to reassess their personal and career goals. The book is easy to read and the concepts readily practiced. If everyone would take the initiative to implement the concepts in this book, the world's happiness quotient would increase dramatically!"

Katherine "Kitty" C. Green, president/CEO of
The Bonita Bay Group

"This book's Four-Dimensional Thinking will change the way you think, and more importantly it will force you to take action. If there's one book to read that will immediately impact your life, it's this one!"

Cameron Johnson, entrepreneur and author of
You Call the Shots

"If you don't know the answers to the questions posed in this book's title, you now have a how-to for finding them. The fascinating real-life stories will inspire you personally and professionally, no matter what your age or stage in life."

Harvey Mackay, author of the *New York Times* best seller
Swim With the Sharks Without Being Eaten Alive

"Reading *Who Are You and What Do You Want?* is like walking through vast vaults of buried treasure—only the cascading gemstones here are all insights into your own life. If you're interested in self-discovery, Ukleja and Lorber are the best tour guides you could wish for."

John David Mann, co-author of *The Go-Giver* and
You Call the Shots

"Ukleja and Lorber tackle the most universal problem faced by postmodern humans, fulfilling our psychological needs. Their organized and simple approach will be useful to readers seeking new paths leading to what Maslow called self-actualization more than a half century ago."

Stephen M. Pfeiffer, Ph.D., Executive Director of The
Association for the Advancement of Psychology

"Read this book, take the 48-hour Who Are You and What Do You Want? personal retreat, and come away feeling like a winner!"

Gary Player, Grand Slam golf champion

"The job for all of us who take pride in helping our clients find their 'sweet spots' has just been made easier. This book encourages readers to assess their strengths, passions, hopes, and desires and to use the answers to guide their own career/life paths. How refreshing to read a blueprint for positive change!"

Susan Silvano, president and CEO, Career
Management International

"I really love this book! For anyone who has a desire to get somewhere in this world, here is a plan for you to follow."

Mike Snegg, president/CEO, Coldwell Banker Grass
Roots Realty; chairman/managing partner, Berkeley
Partners LLC

"The authors are excellent communicators! They use wonderful examples to illustrate how to achieve more from our lives. Following these principles will enable us to be better husbands, wives, parents, friends, and contributors to society. My boys have to read this!"

Lanny Wadkins, 1977 PGA champion, 1995 U.S.
Ryder Cup team captain

"I have always taught that success can be achieved by each one of us. *Who Are You And What Do You Want?* will help you attain that goal. Bob Lorber and Mick Ukleja provide an excellent life-planning guide for bringing out your best and achieving success."

John Wooden, College Basketball Hall of Fame coach
and player

To Louise Ukleja, who has enriched my life for 35 years. You have been a constant source of encouragement and insight as you have shared a commitment to help others bring out the best in themselves.

Mick

To my life partner and wife of 34 years, Sandy Lorber. I am grateful for your friendship, love, and passion for life that makes this a fabulous Journey for the Best of Our Lives.

Bob

Who Are You
and What Do You Want

A Journey for the
Best of Your Life

MICK UKLEJA, PH.D., and ROBERT L. LORBER, PH.D.

Meredith₀ Books
Des Moines, Iowa

Meredith Books
1716 Locust Street
Des Moines, Iowa 50309-3023
meredithbooks.com

Printed in the United States of America.

Library of Congress Control Number: 2007938174
ISBN: 9780696238925

Who Are You and What Do You Want?

A Journey for the Best of Your Life

Foreword

I'm excited about writing the foreword to *Who Are You and What Do You Want?* for two reasons.

First of all, I'm a big fan of Mick Ukleja and Bob Lorber. I've known Mick for ten years. He was a very successful pastor in Orange County and now he's using his skills in other areas. He and his wife founded the Ukleja Center for Ethical Leadership at Long Beach State University, where he invites leaders like myself, John Wooden, Patrick Lencioni and others to share their points of view with students. Mick has a weekly television show and he's one of the finest people I know. I've known Bob for over thirty years. He co-authored *Putting The One Minute Manager to Work* with me. He's on the board of directors for The Ken Blanchard Companies and is one of the best top management team building consultants in the world.

The second reason I'm excited about this book is because I believe that effective leadership is really a transformational journey that includes self leadership, one-on-one leadership, team leadership and organizational leadership. Self leadership comes first, because effective leadership starts on the inside. Before you can hope to lead anyone else, you have to know yourself and what you need to be successful. Only when you have experience in leading yourself are you ready to lead others. The key to one-on-one leadership is being able to develop a trusting relationship with others. If you don't know who you are, or what your strengths and weaknesses are, and are not willing to be vulnerable, you'll never develop a trusting relationship. The same principle applies to team and organizational leadership.

One of the primary mistakes organizations make today is that they spend most of their time and energy trying to solve problems at an organizational level with leaders who haven't asked themselves the fundamental question: Who am I, and what do I want?

This book is about authentic self-leadership and being true to yourself. Why is the question "Who am I?" so difficult to answer? Perhaps because people don't take the time to reflect on their lives—they're too busy just doing, doing, doing. We have to remember that we're not human doings, we are human beings. This book will help you reflect on your life so that you have a clear picture of who you are and what you want. This knowledge will become a firm foundation for all your life decisions and choices.

Mick and Bob ask the question, "What do you want?" rather than "what do you need?" Doing what you need takes effort and struggle and isn't very motivating. Take the same need and turn it into a want—now that's motivating and far less an effort. In the end more of us prefer to do what we want to do rather than what we need to do.

I think you're going to enjoy the Four-Dimensional journey that Mick and Bob will take you on in the pages that follow. You'll start by discovering who you are, then move on to finding out where you are and why you're there. Then you'll explore what you'll do and how you'll do it. Finally, you'll find out who your allies are and how they can help you. This Four-Dimensional roadmap will guide you all the time, allowing you the perspective and clarity to successfully deal with all situations as they arise.

The whole book comes together powerfully at the end when Bob and Mick present the design for a weekend retreat that you can do by yourself, or with friends or business associates. If you can answer the questions in a thoughtful way, you'll come out a better person, because you will know who you are, what you're doing, and what's going to guide your journey.

Ken Blanchard, coauthor of *The One Minute Manager*® and *The One Minute Entrepreneur*™

Introduction

"Another night of missing time with my family," Bob thought as he drove home to Orange County from a meeting with a client in Los Angeles. It had been a productive meeting with a valued client, but after two hours of bumper-to-bumper traffic, he knew both girls would be asleep by the time he walked in the door. "I love my work, I love my clients, I love my business team, and I keep saying how much I love my family, but something is missing," he thought..

Bob and his partner, Kef Kamai, had built a wonderful management consulting firm during 20 successful years. Their team of almost 50 consultants and staff worked with companies all over the world, and they were having a ball. Bob lived in a beautiful home in Villa Park and had a beach house in Laguna Beach. He and his wife were connected to their community, involved in charitable organizations they enjoyed. Everything on the surface was working; everything seemed to be going great; they were living the American dream. But he had a growing knot in his stomach Why? he wondered.

After many months of thinking, one night he sat down with his partner, Kef, and his wife, Sandy, and said, "It's time for a change. I have to do this differently." To his surprise they both admitted feeling the same way. They were all experiencing the growing pressure of the Southern California lifestyle: a commute that had grown from 15 minutes to an hour twice a day, multiplying demands on their time and energy, dwindling satisfaction in what their lives had become. The people whom were truly important to them and truly valued were being pushed aside.

The three of them started talking over dinners to clarify what they really wanted to do and where they might want to go to become more effective at their work and yet have time to enjoy their families. There were many obstacles to making a change: leaving friends, family (Bob's mom and dad lived in Orange County), a great staff, a successful firm, clients, community involvement, schools, a familiar network of services (the bank, pharmacy, doctor, dentist), homes, the beaches, the weather—the list seemed almost endless. But they all agreed it was time for a new dream, which began to take shape: a small town, smaller schools for the kids, community involvement, a university nearby.

Perhaps by now you've guessed this is the story of one of this book's authors, Robert. Scared to death, yet at the same time excited by the possibilities of a change, he and Sandy made the move from Orange County to Davis in northern California. Bob and his partner, Kef, rebuilt their consulting business. The joy of seeing his daughters (ages 7 and 3 at the time) settle into a new home (plus a third daughter who was born after the move) made the move worth it. Certainly in the early stages there were times when he asked himself, "What have I done?" But the difficulties faded with the satisfaction of a new lifestyle that matched what he valued most.

The choices are yours

On the journey to success and happiness in life, it's easy to become frustrated at the inevitable crossroads and detours. Some people give up before they get started; others become discouraged when the journey becomes difficult or complex; still others grow excited by the challenges. Some men and women pass by every opportunity that comes their way because they don't see the inherent possibilities. Like the man who was overheard at his school reunion saying, "If I knew those years would be the best years of my life, I would have had more fun!" Many women and men have enviable careers and relationships yet wish they were somewhere else doing something else with someone else, while others feel happy and successful no matter where they are or whom they're with. Why? Is life that complicated?

Our answer is no, it's not complicated, but life does require making choices. You can choose the path you take in life, but only you can make the choices to take you there. What we hope to accomplish as the authors of this book is to help you discover your path and make better choices. In our consulting work we help people discover their own creative gifts, talents, and passions by guiding them to see what makes them unique. Once they identify what is uniquely their own, it's much easier for them to pursue the best of their life for the rest of their life!

Over the past 30 years working both individually and together, we've had the privilege of mentoring, counseling, and consulting thousands of entrepreneurs, employees, teams, managers, executives, CEOs, and chairmen across corporate America. The priceless insights of our family members, friends, students, colleagues, and parishioners have broadened our quest to discover the traits that happy and successful people share in their personal and family lives as well as at work. After all if you don't feel great at work, you won't at home either, and vice versa. As one 34-year-old executive said to us, "I'm getting a B at work and a C-minus at home. I refuse to think I'm becoming mediocre. Is it the job, or is it me?"

More than mediocre

No one we know has ever had a goal to be mediocre, yet that's what happens when people compromise themselves in a world driven by hyperkinetic activity where we feel like we have to compartmentalize our work, home, personal, and spiritual lives, like actors on a rotating stage in the play *Stop the World—I Want to Get Off*. What we all desperately need is a way to step off the stage, take a seat in the balcony, and look at the big picture, the whole stage, the scenery, the plot. Or to change metaphors, we need to kick the cord out of the treadmill.

Our combined experiences have inspired us to find the common threads in those people we've met who are noticeably happy and successful. From those observations we have developed a way to uncover one's uniqueness called Four-Dimensional Thinking. It integrates all the moving, shifting, and conjoining goals in your life onto the same page; it makes tangible your deepest dreams and highest aspirations.

Four-Dimensional Thinking provides a model for self-reflection, a plan for life planning. Each dimension is created by questions that provoke reflection—reflection that will draw out your unique talents and passions, the essence of who you really are. Each dimension is further developed by more questions—questions that lead to the answers to create a life map to guide you to the best of your life.

Why so many questions? Often asking a question is more valuable than the answer. But not just any question, the right question. Some can lead you in the wrong direction or in no direction in particular. A useful question will focus your attention on what's truly important and bring important truths about you to the surface. The Four-Dimensional process is not about putting information into your life; it's about discovering what's already within you. Learning from other people is certainly important; learning about yourself, from yourself, is even more important. You can become your own teacher, your own mentor, who's always available to teach the next lesson.

In the chapters that follow, the Four Dimensions are integrated with and dependent upon the others. Each dimension is integrated with and complements the other three. You live in four dimensions: height, width, depth, and time. Einstein called it the space–time continuum. In similar fashion the best of your life is lived in Four Dimensions.

The First Dimension asks, "Who are you and what do you want?" The answer takes you to the core of your personal strengths, passions, and dreams. It breaks through and clears away any imagination gridlock that keeps you from living the best of your life.

The Second Dimension asks, "Where are you and why are you there?" Once you understand how you have arrived at where you are right now you can create your own life map. You can review your past choices, identify faulty assumptions that have gone undetected, and clarify positive approaches that are worth repeating.

The Third Dimension asks, "What will you do and how will you do it?" It's great to dream, but whenever dreams collide with reality, reality wins. This dimension offers you a direction to ensure a more successful journey.

The Fourth Dimension asks, "Who are your allies and how can they help?" Relationships with family, friends, and coworkers are indispensable. Flying solo for long stretches of time isn't safe or fun. No one accomplishes anything that leads to lasting satisfaction by himself or herself. This dimension explores how to build the kind of relationships that benefit everyone involved.

Over the years, we have presented the Four-Dimensional life-planning process to hundreds of people in every stage of life. When we talk to high school students, they tell us that no one has ever asked them these questions before. Usually, astute teenagers tell us, when they are asked what they want to do in life, the questioner is really looking for the "right" answer, ready to tell them what they "should" do.

When we lead classes with M.B.A. students, the questions they ask are not about business skills or leadership strategies; they are primarily life-planning questions. On the verge of launching their professional careers with nothing to hold them back from going anywhere they want, they are asking, "How can I know what I will ultimately enjoy? How can I find more than just a job? I think I know what I want to do, but how will I get there?"

Working professionals often tell us that they don't have too many choices left. They fear they are running out of time to make career changes. Yet they feel stuck in what they are doing, hemmed in by years on a particular career path. One successful dentist told us, "I really hate being a dentist, but I'm making $200,000 a year, and I don't know what else I can do. If I quit what would I do?"

Breaking down the barriers
As a pastor Mick encouraged people to follow their dreams, advising them to combine their strengths and passions and sync them into a plan of action. Yet one day as Mick stood at the pulpit in front of the 2,500-member church he had pastored from its small beginnings, a thought raced through his mind: "What am I still doing here?"

For the previous five years he had been speaking on the subject of leadership to numerous groups, businesses, nonprofit organizations, and schools. The opportunity to speak to the business and personal lives of corporate and organizational leaders was becoming more and more rewarding for him. It enabled him to influence men and women who in turn could influence others through their ethical behavior and leadership practices. However, there was a tug on his shoulder saying, "Are you crazy? You've been here 20 years!

It's become just what you envisioned, the congregation keeps growing, and you love them—each and every one. And they love you. Why would you leave now, just when it's getting comfortable?"

This inner struggle wasn't new; it had been going on in Mick's head for several years. The barriers seemed huge. What about the future of this wonderful congregation? Who would take the church to the next level? What about the pain of letting go of something he built from its infancy and watching it grow? How would he cope with those who might feel betrayed or abandoned by his departure? What about the numerous opportunities for misunderstanding his intentions? Some may confuse his change as a lack of commitment; the majority, he trusted, would see it for what it was: a reinvention of himself and an opportunity for him to grow and touch the lives of others in a new, dynamic way.

The challenge became more important to Mick than being comfortable with the status quo. As he had told those who sought his advice when faced with personal change, "A veneer can stay. But slowly it begins to atrophy—eventually leaving nothing but an empty shell." Going into the corporate world and using his talents to encourage personal growth in leaders was becoming his passion.

He decided to follow his own advice and made the move. His transition was planned carefully—painful at first but in the end positive not only for him but also for those he was leaving. His former congregation benefited by learning from a new pastor with a new vision for the future. In the following years, the congregation grew significantly. Meanwhile Mick continues to expand the size of his new "congregation" through meetings, seminars, and speaking with business and political leaders about how they can better affect the people around them. Through their roles as leaders they ultimately improve the world around them.

A compass to guide you

Detailed life maps are not what we offer; instead we give you a compass and show you how easy and reliable it is to use. The journey for the best of your life takes focus, determination, discipline, and guts. It doesn't just happen. Although many successful people we've worked with make their successes seem effortless, it looks easy because they intentionally think and behave at a Four-Dimensional level.

Your identity—knowing who you are—and your accomplishments—having what you want—are secondary on the trip you take through life. It's the people you meet and love, the relationships and the experiences you have along the way that make life worth living.

Enjoy your own journey and the best of your life!

Mick Ukleja and Bob Lorber

Chapter 1

Your Journey Begins With a Destination

"Would you tell me please, which way I ought to go from here?"

"That depends a good deal on where you want to get to," said the Cat.

"I don't much care where—" said Alice.

"Then it doesn't matter which way you go," said the Cat.

"—so long as I get somewhere," Alice added as an explanation.

"Oh, you're sure to do that," said the Cat, "if you only walk long enough."

Lewis Carroll's *Alice's Adventures in Wonderland*

Mark was a successful entrepreneur who "had it made." Great wife, great kids, beautiful home, good health. His real estate business in Florida was growing rapidly. He had his life wired in every respect, or so he thought.

"I was working really hard building a career and had everything cranked up to light speed. Then one day at my office my assistant Emily brought in an unopened FedEx envelope, gingerly placed it on my desk, and quickly left the room. Must be important, I thought, wondering why Emily didn't open it and why she shut the door behind her. I looked at the return address and noticed something rather odd—it was my home address and the envelope was from my wife, Laura. My mind raced to a worst-case scenario. Then I realized that in the worst scenario an envelope would be hand-delivered from an attorney's office—not from Laura!

"As I opened the letter, my imagination ran wild. It's not every day you get a FedEx from your spouse. The letter began: 'Dear Mark: I'm writing this letter because it's hard to get your attention these days.' Laura went on to describe some of the important parts of our life that I was ignoring because of my myopic concentration on my business. 'The pressures of higher education, career, and a growing family can camouflage an eroding marriage relationship,' she wrote.

"Eroding marriage! Ouch. She had my attention.

" 'A drifting marriage can give the appearance of success, but in it dwells the seeds of a failing marriage. It's like two trains going in the same direction yet on different tracks. The genuine survival of our marriage demands that we both get on the same train, on the same track.' "

Somewhere along the way Mark got lost. He drifted off course and didn't realize it.

He's not alone.

Many people feel at a deep level that their lives should be different from what they're living right now. They have a yearning for something more. Young people with high-powered high finance or technology jobs are working 70 hours a week with salaries well into the six figures, yet they don't know what they want and wonder how they can stop long enough to find out. Middle-aged men and women talk about what they have had to give up in order to make a living to support their families; struggling simply to keep their heads above water consumes almost all their time and energy.

Successful CEOs say they don't know what they will do when they retire because their identities are completely tied up with their corporate positions. Busy entrepreneurs say they feel trapped by the endless list of decisions they face, no matter whether they're at work or at home. And when they finally seem to have the financial wherewithal to do what they want, they say their businesses would suffer if they took time off to think about life. For them the old adage sums it up well: When you're dancing with a gorilla, you can't stop dancing until the gorilla decides to stop. Even retired entrepreneurs who have sold their businesses say they'd like to begin living a more meaningful life but they can't really name their destination. They have never before reflected on life at a deeper level, and now they find the process completely foreign and intimidating. Yet all these people journey on with the hope that somehow they can find what they're sure is something better somewhere.

For some the problem is they haven't taken the time to clearly determine their destination in life. Like Alice in Wonderland they are just trying to get somewhere. But like the saying "If you aim at nothing you're sure to hit it every time," they are aiming at nowhere and bound to arrive there.

For many others the problem is not so much a lack of destination. They have at least a sense of where they want to arrive in life. They know it includes happiness and success in some shape or form. The problem is that they've wandered off course. And often they don't even realize they've lost their way.

What you have is not who you are

Many people in Western nations today suffer from unipolar depression—having bad feelings without a specific cause. The incidence of all types of depression today is an epidemic. The World Health Organization (WHO) estimates that 100 million people in the United States, Canada, and the European Union are clinically depressed. In the United States the impact is $83 billion a year in mental health costs and lost productivity.

Sociological studies show that as income rises so does the sense of well-being, but only so far. Once middle-class level is reached, money and happiness are no longer directly correlated as satisfaction goals and milestones keep moving. People's needs and wants grow and become intertwined. Food, clothing, and shelter can be bought, but once acquired they are no longer needs. Wants may never be satisfied, no matter how many times those desires are fulfilled. The more you have, the more you seem to want. Some people try to justify buying expensive things as an "investment," but consider how easily last year's must-haves are today's "fashion don'ts." Things will not produce satisfaction.

In *Trading Up: Why Consumers Want New Luxury Goods* by Michael J. Silverstein and Neil Fiske, a survey of consumers shows a country full of overwhelmed, isolated, lonely, worried, and unhappy Americans.[1]

Never have enough time	**54.8%**
Don't get enough sleep	**53.8%**
Don't spend enough time with friends	**51.5%**
Worry about my health	**40.1%**
Working harder than ever	**39.0%**
Feel a great deal of stress in my life	**36.6%**
Don't feel appreciated for all that I do	**36.5%**
Am happy with my appearance	**30.5%**
Am happy in my romantic relationships	**17.8%**

Despite expanding purchasing power and consumer knowledge combined with an almost limitless assortment of goods and services at their disposal, only 39 percent agreed with the statement "I have the right balance in my life"; only 37 percent with the statement "I feel like a part of my community"; and only 35 percent—that's about one in three people—with the statement "I have a lot of close friends." What's going on?

In his book The Progress Paradox, Gregg Easterbrook describes Western nations as having "more of everything except happiness." He points to studies that show lacking money can lead to unhappiness, but having it does not cause happiness. Millionaires are no happier than people of average income. For most people happiness increases with age. The disabled and chronically ill report a slightly higher sense of well-being than the population at large; they have a higher appreciation for the value of their own lives.[2]

> The key to any successful
> and enjoyable journey is
> a planned destination.

Having a summer house in the Hamptons, in Malibu, or on the Riviera; a six-, seven-, or eight-figure income; and a limo or jet at your disposal doesn't create happiness. New living arrangements, five-figure square footages, possessions, and status may quickly become nothing more than a momentarily revised status quo. Something that looks better always comes along.

Changing destinations, or not

Doug and his wife, a retired couple in their seventies, live in a 1950s bungalow with river frontage in Ketchum, Idaho. One day their friend Rebecca stopped to talk with Doug, who was mowing his front lawn. "How do you like the new place going up?" she asked. Next to them builders were completing a 9,000-square-foot house. Doug stopped his hand mower by the street, smiled, and replied, "It's quite a change, and now my property is more valuable than I ever dreamed possible. We're offered $2 million for our place on a regular basis. The real estate agents say that whoever buys it will tear down the house and build one like the one going up next door. Our tax assessment went up so much that I asked my wife, 'Should we just sell and take the money to do and go where we want or stay and pay the tax increase?' We talked about it, considered where we'd go and what we'd do. Then we looked at our view of the mountains and the river below, which were the reasons we bought the property in the first place—for $50,000 back in the 1950s, and we both started laughing about the sheer craziness of it all! Then my wife said that if we left here she'd miss waking up with the sun over the eastern mountain ridges and the sound of the river below. I said I'd miss seeing the elk, deer, and red fox as we have our coffee on the porch. Together we realized that no one could pay us enough to move away from what we have right here."

Rebecca asked, "Did it annoy you when the agents said your home would be torn down by the next owner?"

"Nah—not at all," Doug answered. "At some point in time every house is a teardown." He pointed to the new construction. "Even my new neighbor's beautiful place will be a teardown eventually. It's all just a matter of time."

Time and place

As any pilot will tell you, if you take off from Los Angeles and want to land at New York's JFK airport yet are off only one compass degree to the north—you'll end up somewhere in White Plains,

New York, about 26 miles away. Just one degree—that's 0.2 percent—and you have committed what the FAA calls a "gross navigational error." Stray off course only 5 degrees—barely 1 percent off—and you arrive in Albany, 126 miles away from New York. A seemingly small decision becomes a larger issue as you travel farther and farther.

The same thing can happen in your life. You start your journey. You think you know where you're going. And then the next thing you know, you're in Albany. You've misjudged your direction just a little. You've made daily choices. But the sum total of small vector changes has landed you far from where you want to be.

Being human we all have a tendency to drift off course. That's inevitable. But getting off course actually isn't the problem. Failing to make midcourse corrections is the problem.

When NASA sends a space shuttle on a mission, in-flight corrections are expected. That's why the spacecraft has rocket motors to adjust its course. Even a satellite launched into geosynchronous orbit—in effect staying in the same place relative to the Earth—has motors to adjust its flight based on feedback from tracking stations on earth.

Even the most sophisticated guidance systems, however, which can make hundreds of adjustments based on clear and accurate feedback, don't serve much purpose if NASA engineers have no idea what the ideal orbit is. In other words, without a specific destination all the midcourse corrections in the world are pointless efforts. Anyone, including highly successful people, can find himself or herself headed in the wrong direction, stuck on the wrong course. For a successful journey have a clear picture of your destination, recognize when you're on the wrong course, and enact course corrections to be sure you reach your desired destination.

Making course corrections

With the letter from his wife in hand, Mark realized he needed a course correction. "That hit me upside the head. At first I felt helpless—I had been so focused on what I was doing with my career that I didn't have any idea how I was going to bring balance into my life. I had ignored many important things to focus on one. Laura was right: I didn't include her in my life. I had prioritized my job over my connections with her, the kids, our parents and siblings, and friends. My life felt like someone was turning up the speed on the treadmill. I had confused focus with myopia and was missing the most important elements for successful living.

"Laura's letter compelled me to cancel my lunch date that day. Going to a nearby park with a pad of paper, PDA, and finding a bench beneath a tree, right away it was as if my pen exploded onto the page. Before me spilled dreams and goals that had long been beneath my radar of my consciousness: *Begin today to show Laura how important she is to me; spend more intimate and uninterruptible time with my family and good friends; make more personal connections with people—especially those closest to me; it is up to me to make my life work.* By merely sitting there in the park, the sense of urgency and stress level that had been my daily state of mind lifted. Having the list right in front of me in my own handwriting made me realize how far I had drifted away from my values. It became clear to me what was important in my life, as opposed to the things I was chasing after. Seeing that more clearly made all the difference.

"Who is waiting for bad news? For sure I wasn't ready to hear what Laura wrote to me in her letter, but there was no way to run away from the reality of our diminishing relationship. Truth is powerful, but only if you allow yourself to be guided by it, right?

I was willing to make any course corrections to keep Laura and regain the life we had planned together. Too much was at stake not to pay attention. I never felt so loved in all my life! That afternoon my wonderful, loving wife received two dozen yellow roses and a message from me that said, 'Thank you, Laura. I needed that!' "

Being true to yourself

"Who are you and what do you want?"

In our consulting practices we've asked that question to a lot of people. Some are immediately uncomfortable. They don't even like to hear the question, much less try to answer it. Yet most of the people we meet with are thoroughly intrigued with the idea of really knowing themselves and figuring out the reason they're living.

"Who am I?" It's a very simple question, yet some people avoid answering it their entire lives. "What do I want?" The answer can get blurry and change from day to day when it's not clearly defined. Some feel safer and more comfortable reacting to change rather than creating or managing it. Is it because they don't know the answer? Or is it because they fear the answer?

Some people say they avoid going for a medical checkup. Is it because they're afraid of finding out their health condition is serious, or is it because they know they will need to alter their lifestyle to be healthy? Their doctor may advise losing weight, exercising more, eating healthier, limiting drinking, and stopping smoking.

Answering truthfully the question, "Who are you?" forces you to get right to the point: What is the point of my life? What is my purpose? Some men or women tell us they already know who they are and what they want; yet when we probe a little deeper they admit, "OK, I am stumped for a specific answer." Answering the question is like exploring new territory.

When the great explorers like Magellan, Columbus, and Vespucci sailed to new worlds, they had no maps or their maps were dangerously unreliable. They used the North Star to navigate because it was the one constant they could rely on. Likewise there are no maps for you to follow on the journey of your life. But you do have a North Star by which to navigate: Your North Star is being true to yourself.

Answering both "Who are you?" and "What do you want?" will help you set destinations you can reach. The questions help you recognize the course corrections you need. Answering the questions untruthfully, however, always lead to disaster.

Truth is a reliable constant. It eliminates distractions and clutter, clarifies every situation, and helps you manage any change you want to make. By making course corrections you satisfy dreams, hopes, and aspirations. Being truthful with yourself becomes your navigational tool to stay on course. Being truthful becomes an internal compass, automatically pointing you in the right direction. A commitment to the truth about yourself always serve you well, even in uncharted waters with unexpected weather.

Reflection is the only effective way to bridge from the past to the future.

Through all the challenges, changes, and transitions in life, one thing should be standard operating procedure: Be true to yourself. Truth has an immediate and lasting impact on your personal and business relationships. When truth is your personal ally, three things happen immediately:

First you feel better about yourself. You travel light, without the baggage of phoniness or a hidden past. Second you have less stress and conflict in your life; you don't have the fallout that eventually catches up to people who lie to themselves and others. Third you have integrity and are respected by the people who count. You are part of many communities—work, family, neighborhood, and more. Knowing who you are and what you want in life, supported by truth in all your relationships, will help you reach your destination.

Most people avoid thinking deeply about who they are and what they want because it might mean altering their present to improve their future. Yet reflection is a very effective way to bridge from the past to the future. However, it doesn't minimize the need for action. As management expert and author Henry Mintzberg wrote in the Harvard Business Review, "Action without reflection is thoughtless. Reflection without action is passive."[3]

That's why so often it takes a crisis point—like a special delivery letter from a spouse, or more—to make us stop and reflect.

Taking a time out

On September 7, 2001, as a copilot for United Airlines, Cholene Espinoza flew the approach above Manhattan past the World Trade Center towers. The next day she received orders to fly from New York to San Francisco on the morning of September 11. At the last minute she was rescheduled from the ill-fated United Airlines Flight 93. Watching the horrific news on television that day, she was overcome with grief for those in the Twin Towers, which she had flown by only a few nights before, and the heroic passengers and crew aboard Flight 93.

"The enormity of the 'what ifs' and the loss of humanity was overwhelming," Cholene said. "Why me? And why had I survived several other near-fatal situations? It was deeper than survivor's guilt. For me it was time to start thinking about the fragility and preciousness of life, define who I was, know what I really wanted, and ensure I was living to the fullest my own life and not someone else's. I wanted to live up to the second, third, even fourth chances at life given to me. I requested and was granted a three-month leave from my job."

Cholene hit the pause button, regrouped, and reset her pace in life to reflect what she truly valued. In the end she realized how much she loved her work as a pilot. She continued flying and found a way to satisfy the keen obligation she felt to give back to others by establishing in the wake of Hurricane Katrina a nonprofit academy to educate children.

> When you have clarity about your destination, you lead yourself— instead of allowing other people, events, or situations to lead you.

What gets in the way of knowing who you are and what you want? The short answer is: You do. You get in your own way. But when you have clarity about your destination, you lead yourself. You do not allow other people, events, or situations to lead you. As leadership pioneer Warren Bennis says, "You become authentic. The word 'authentic' has as its root the word 'author.' You become the author of your life rather than a copy or shadow of someone else's. Authenticity is all about living your life to reflect what you say is important to you."

The road is not always easy, but if you know who you are, then what you want tends to show up.

Changing destinations

Steve Hadley was looking for direction when he met Mick, then senior pastor of a fast-growing church in Southern California. "From the time I was 9 years old," Steve recalls, "I had a love for helping animals. We always had a lot of animals around when I was growing up, so several experiences helped shape my passion for veterinary medicine. Later while managing a veterinary emergency referral practice, I learned that I also loved the management side of my work and felt challenged to do something about it. That led me to enroll in the Executive M.B.A. program at Pepperdine University. One degree requirement was to complete a strategy project. That's what led me to Mick.

"At church I was listening to Mick speak on the topic of following your dreams and passions. 'Who are you and what do you want?' kept reverberating in my brain. As silly as it might have seemed, my dream was to create a world-class aquarium in Southern California. Instead of discouraging me from what many might have thought was an outlandish ambition, Mick challenged me to figure out how to make my dream a reality. He said a dream is like an airplane: A lot of people can fly a plane once it's in the air, but landing it is quite another story. He asked me to figure out how to land it—he asked me, 'What will you do and how will you do it? Who are your allies and how can they help?'

"I started my investigation and discovered that certain local events were already in motion that might make the idea of an aquarium fall on very receptive ears. Pieces of my plan were coming together and I took the plunge into the aquarium project! Within three months I had resigned from my position, pulled out of the M.B.A. program, founded a not-for-profit corporation to develop the master plan for an aquarium, and secured six acres of land in the city of Long Beach. And while all this was going on, my wife, Denise, and I became parents. Wow!

"Once I was focused, moving forward seemed pretty easy, but the initial period of activity was followed by 18 months where nothing seemed to be happening. It was important for me to know what I wanted and where I was. This gave me the resilience to tweak my plan and to keep going. There were serious moments of losing faith: The economy was bad, and I was personally funding the initial efforts, which was seriously impacting our family finances."

Once Steve had a team in place to develop the aquarium, he decided to finish his M.B.A. He completed his degree at the Wharton School and went to work in San Francisco for Goldman Sachs, which had underwritten the revenue bonds for the aquarium.

But something still wasn't right. Steve felt stuck. "Banking? Is this the outcome? Banking was not my passion! What was I doing putting on a suit at 4 a.m. and working on the 30th floor of the Bank of America building in downtown San Francisco? How did I get here? Suddenly my life wasn't making any sense to me."

Through the years, Steve and Mick had stayed in touch. "What would your life look like if you weren't stuck?" Mick asked him. "What would your life look like if it made sense? Where did you lose sight of your destination?"

A short time later on Halloween night, the answer stood in front of Steve. "As we were preparing for Halloween, my oldest son, Nathan, wanted to dress up as a veterinarian. It was the image of him in my blue surgical scrubs with the embroidered 'Dr. Hadley' on the pocket, holding several stuffed animals with bandages on them, that reconnected me with my real passion."

Steve reflected on the sequence of events in his life and realized that he hadn't left the veterinary industry because he didn't like being a veterinarian. He loved management too and was duly trained in finances. How could he combine all his strengths with his passion? After some research he resigned from his banking job and joined the Veterinary Centers of America (VCA). VCA had grown in six years from 11 hospitals to 175 hospitals. Steve joined the group and was given responsibility for 45 of those hospitals. As vice president of VCA, he is now combining his strengths in business management and finance with his love for animals.

> ## If you know who you are, then what you want tends to show up.

Fine-tuning your destination

You can land exactly where you want and you can become all you want to be by charting your own course and reviewing your checklist before takeoff. The weight of your cargo is a very important factor in taking off and landing. How heavy is your emotional baggage? Do you have enough stamina or discipline to complete the trip? Are you fueled with your own set of values? Is your personal integrity stowed securely aboard? How will you be nourished during your journey—physically, emotionally, mentally, and spiritually? Who is your copilot? Does your crew have the same destination? If they don't want to go where you're going, what will be compromised? What is your estimated time of arrival? Making stops along the way means it will take longer to get to your destination. Is there a faster way? What will you do after you get there? A destination of happiness and success is attainable only with persistence because it takes some effort to figure yourself out! The truth about who you are and what you want is your guide, making the journey to your destination safe and enjoyable.

You are the pilot in command, master of your life.

It all begins with your destination.

For Reflection

Personal destination setting and planning

The more you know about yourself, the more you will learn from yourself and your experiences. People who have a destination clearly in mind and are working a purposeful plan toward it are the ones who experience the best of their lives. Now that you've started thinking about your destination, here are some questions for further reflection. Your answers will help you prepare for your personal Who Am I and What Do I Want? retreat, which is described in detail as the final chapter of this book.

1. If I received a special delivery letter from someone reminding me of something important in my life that I was forgetting, what would that letter say?

2. If I could make a change and be assured of succeeding, how would my life be different from the life I am living right now?

3. During the past year which work-related activities did I enjoy most? Why? Which family-related activities? Why? Which personal activities? Why?

4. When do I take the time to reflect on my life? How do I take the time to reflect on my life?

5. Which action, if I did it immediately, would have the greatest positive effect on my life?

Chapter 2

How Much Truth Are You Willing to Tell?

All truths are easy to understand once they
are discovered; the point is to discover them.

Galileo Galilei

As college basketball's win-
ningest head coach, sports icon John Wooden set the bar so high
there is little chance anyone will be able to match his record of
accomplishment. He is the first and one of only three people in the
Basketball Hall of Fame enshrined as both a collegiate player and
coach. Under Wooden's guidance the UCLA Bruins set all-time re-

cords with four 30-0 seasons, 88 consecutive victories, 38 straight NCAA tournament victories, 20 PAC 10 championships, and 10 national championships, including 7 in a row. He did all of this without ever losing sight of who he was or what he wanted. As he approaches age 100, this inspirational teacher continues to live life in the present, focused on a destination he set many years ago.

Coach Wooden's father taught him and his brothers what his father called "the two sets of three" for living their lives.

The first set was about being honest with others:

> Never lie
>
> Never cheat
>
> Never steal

The second set was about being honest with ourselves:

> No whining
>
> No complaining
>
> No excuses

"Dad's two sets of threes were a compass for me to do the right thing and behave in a proper manner," Wooden said. They clearly laid the foundation for an incredible string of successes both on and off the court.

In addition to following these rules, Wooden carries a copy of a handwritten, seven-item creed that his father gave him when he graduated from grade school in Centerton, Indiana. The item at the top of his list:

"Be true to yourself."

Coach Wooden's advice on living a successful life is focused and concise: "Perhaps you fret and think you can't make a difference in the way things are. Wrong. You can make the biggest difference of all. You can change yourself. And when you do that, you become a very powerful and important force."

In order to change be truthful with yourself—not truth in the abstract or philosophically or in a vacuum. It's all about being honest with yourself. Usually when people speak of telling the truth, they mean being truthful with other people. That's highly commendable. But of even more fundamental importance is speaking the truth to yourself.

That's easier said than done. It's easy to tell yourself something other than the unvarnished truth. Self-deception is, well, deceptive. Even when you insist you are standing for the truth, you can easily slip into less-than-truthful mode. Do you ever hear yourself saying things like this:

> "This one doesn't count."
>
> "Just this once."
>
> "If you only knew...."
>
> "I did it for you (or the kids, or the company, or the shareholders, or...)."
>
> "I'm not always...."
>
> "That's easy for you, but I ...."

Such phrases are signals you are making excuses or, rather, excusing yourself from the truth.

Lying to yourself is at best counterproductive and at worst destructive. Telling yourself the unvarnished truth is the most liberating action you can take. It's not always easy, and in some cases it might even be painful. But the results are both freeing and energizing. When you are honest with yourself, you have a clear connection between the problems you face and the happiness you experience. Avoiding the truth is like using the wrong map: You'll never reach your destination because you won't know the reality of where you are or where you're headed.

Who is the leader?

Many people don't see themselves as leaders. When they think of leadership, the first thing that comes to their mind is someone else leading others. Invite a group of kindergartners into a game of Follow the Leader and ask who wants to be the leader, and they will all jump up shouting enthusiastically, "Me! Me!" But go down the street to a middle school or high school and ask, "Who are the leaders here?" and the response is usually blank stares. Some students may look around the room for their teacher, or others may point to the class president or the captain of a sports team.

> "You can make the biggest difference of all. You can change yourself." —John Wooden

What happened over those years to take away the energy, passion, and willingness to enjoy the feeling of being a leader? When did the change begin to occur in those students? When did they stop seeing themselves as leaders? When did they become passive followers? What happened?

They simply became "adult-erated"—contaminated by the way they choose to think about themselves. It started the moment they began to worry what others were thinking about them. They started conforming when they began to worry about what kind of lunch box they carried, the clothes they wore, or who liked or didn't like them. Slowly but surely, looking like, talking like, dressing like their classmates became their overriding goal. Sadly this kind of subversive self-sabotage begins as early as the first grade. Is it possible to get back that childlike enthusiasm? It is, but first you have to be willing to be childlike.

Leadership is the ability to influence others. Self-leadership, then, consists of the thoughts, behaviors, and strategies that help you exert influence over yourself. You create the biggest barriers to your personal success and happiness when you care more about what others think than you care about what you think. The key to self-leadership is being honest with yourself. The more you truly know yourself, the fewer detours you take on the journey to your life's destination.

Self-leadership—the ability to lead yourself—requires confidence to act on your values, no matter what the consequences. It requires the willingness to openly express yourself, no matter how foolish you think you may look to others.

Once you learn to lead yourself, you begin to make a positive and lasting difference. It's the ripple effect. Leaders inspire others to extend themselves far beyond any of their preconceived boundaries and limitations. Great leaders make great things happen because they are committed to their dreams and willing to live by their values at any cost. Their commitment to their values empowers them to change the world around them.

Reactive or proactive?

Whenever you avoid taking charge of your life, you become a reactive machine. When you don't know what you want, you react to everyone else's desires, schedules, invitations, requests, and agendas. Rather than going in the direction of what's best for you and doing what you need to do to make yourself happy and healthy, you give up control of your days, evenings, weekends, months, years—life.

Look at your daily planner. Your current level of self-leadership is reflected in every appointment. Have you scheduled private time to be with your spouse, loved ones, or family on a regular basis? When you have that special time, are the cell phones and pagers turned off? Are you checking emails and text messages? Is that time sacred and uninterruptible? Are there any business and social events or activities you want to do or should do? Is there time to enjoy the things you like, or are you rushing through the day, racing through events and relationships to get to the next one?

What happens when you relinquish control of something as simple as your calendar? You enmesh your life into other people's needs and wants as if your time is of no value. This process becomes pervasive to the point that you may rarely do what you want. The result? You don't exercise power over the direction your life takes; you become stressed, weary, and angry.

> When you don't know what you want, you react to everyone else's desires, schedules, invitations, requests, and agendas.

Rarely do we humans hold ourselves accountable; often we point the finger of blame elsewhere. It's become endemic in our culture to blame others. We blame the boss, the business, employees, coworkers, the media, and the educational, medical, legal, and governmental institutions for the ruts in which we find ourselves. We blame the fashion magazines because we don't like the way we look. We blame the stock and real estate markets for not making us wealthy. We blame our parents, spouse, children, in-laws, or the entire family for our being stuck. All this blaming and avoiding responsibility leads to a negative, frustrated, depressed, litigious, violent, and angry society. It is the antithesis of self-leadership.

Chuck Boppell has spent his entire career in the food service industry, most recently as president and CEO of Worldwide Restaurant Concepts (WRC), which owns and operates the Sizzler and Pat & Oscar's restaurant chains and is a franchisee of 85 KFC restaurants in the United States and Australia.

"Shortly after I arrived at WRC," Chuck recalls, "we had an event in Milwaukee where a Sizzler franchisee had some procedural failures cutting and handling meat and introduced E. coli into the system. I learned a great deal from that experience. When we later had a similar problem at Pat & Oscar's, I was able to apply what I'd learned from that Milwaukee experience as well as draw from my personal beliefs and put together the team that handled the crisis from the beginning until the end. This would not have been a possibility without my own personal emotional growth. The strength and the wisdom I needed were launched from my inner core."

For Boppell averting an even larger crisis meant being completely honest with himself, his team, and the public—customers, media, shareholders, employees, and other stakeholders—despite pressure from company lawyers and other advisers to be less forthcoming with the bad news. "I had lawyers and insurance people telling me I was doing it all wrong," Chuck says. "Instead I said, 'It's our responsibility and here's what's going on.' Our strategy was to be honest and to be out in front telling people what was going on and answering questions and taking responsibility for this problem. We invited the press into our kitchens with their cameras. There was a tremendous amount of pressure for us to back off of this approach—our insurance company was threatening to pull their coverage. They told us point-blank, 'You need to just get your name out of the press and hide! Let it blow over!' Instead our team took the opposite tack, saying to ourselves, 'If we're already on the front page, at least get good mention in along with the bad!' "

Even though the Pat & Oscar's division was hurt by this experience, clearly a focus on strong core values helped the organization defuse a volatile situation. Boppell says, "We're recovering. I would say we're 90 to 95 percent back. What allowed us to recover most of our business so quickly? I believe it was the way we handled it."

How was it that Chuck was able to stay committed to his values and keep his team—and his own life—on track through such a difficult situation? According to Chuck, whom Bob has coached for many years, early in his life a mentor planted the value of personal responsibility in his life. "There was a very special teacher in my high school who lived on my early morning paper route. When I got through, I'd go by and have a cup of coffee and talk with her. At that point in my life, I could duck all the things that were wrong and actually feel that I was in the right and everybody else was screwed up. I wasn't being honest. One morning, out of the blue, she sat me down and said, 'The problem you're having is that you're not taking accountability for all this stuff going on around you—it's never your fault!' That piece of shrapnel has remained lodged in my brain ever since."

Chuck learned early from his mentor how important it is to take total—not partial—responsibility for his life. Self-leadership should be the basis of anyone's decision-making process. In this fast-paced age, too many people allow their lives to be run by a clock instead of a compass—they're slaves to schedules, never quiet or still enough to hear their own voice. Sometimes they let problems and crises take over, as if we are powerless. Problems then become excuses to be angry, overbearing, and stubborn. Self-leadership is the act of mastering moods, attitudes, and actions.

Reacting to symptoms

Underlying problems are not always easy to address, especially if they've been going on for a long time or if you are mirroring the way a parent dealt with issues. The real cause can be difficult to detect, blanketed by years of denial. When you are less than truthful with yourself, you are like a physician who focuses on symptoms alone instead of the fundamental causes of the problem. That can lead to an endless, unproductive, frustrating search for treatments, trying one thing after another, but all the while the patient becomes sicker.

It's not uncommon to become sidetracked or talked into taking a quick and easy fix. A quick fix addresses one thing: a symptom. When you address only a symptom, the underlying problem remains, festers, and worsens. The real problem hides beneath the noise, emotions, and distractions. When there's no real purpose or meaning to your life and only symptoms are treated, the cause of a problem is never addressed. The lack of fulfillment, happiness, or significance may lead to counterproductive behavior. Power, prestige, position, or possessions become ends in themselves, which they were never intended to be. Lack of purpose can also take you in the opposite direction—to a self-destructive life. In either case developing nurturing, lasting relationships becomes impossible.

"It's not my fault" is not self-leadership

It's easy for some people to grow comfortable in the role of a victim when every day seems to be fraught with problems that are never resolved. Nothing is ever their fault. Circumstances are always beyond their control. It's easy for some people to feel they are drowning in one problem after another, manipulating others into becoming the audience for their melodramatic stories of misfortune. They distract themselves and attempt to distract others with their ongoing soap opera. Rather than taking steps to solve a situation, they waste precious time complaining instead of acting, talking instead of doing. Yet using that same energy to tackle one problem at a time will eventually help you reach your destination.

If ever there was a person with a rightful claim to victimhood, it is Melanie Washington. She has experienced many profound losses throughout her life, many more than any one person should have to bear. Yet she has managed to use these negative experiences to create something good in the world. This inspiring woman is founder of the nonprofit youth organization MATFA (Mentoring, A Touch From Above) in Long Beach, California. The program goes inside California Youth Authority detention centers for youths between the ages of 10 and 25 to mentor them, develop them, and help them prepare to reenter society. In the past 10 years, more than 200 young men have participated in MATFA. Of the 30 men in the program who have returned to society from prison, only one has gone back, compared to a state average of some 55 percent. The success has grown out of Melanie's tragedy and her unwillingness to allow herself to sink into victimhood.

At the age of 10, Melanie witnessed the murders of her mother and sister at the hands of her abusive stepfather. Melanie was spared only because his pistol jammed. She blamed herself for their deaths because just a few days prior to the murder, Melanie had revealed to her mother that her stepfather had been sexually abusing her and her sister, so their mother had left him.

"I lived with the burden for many years that their deaths were my fault. I didn't have a life after that. Just a child on this earth, scared about which way to go and mad at myself for telling on my stepfather, and just angry in general. I didn't talk or share anything with anybody or tell on anybody because I was afraid someone I really cared about would die."

At the age of 18, Melanie ran away from home and married her boyfriend. "Two months into my marriage, he was beating on me, but I took the beatings as a punishment for telling on my stepfather. Through two pregnancies he was beating on me, kicking me in the stomach. He gave me hepatitis, and I was in the hospital for 22 days and almost died. After delivering my second child and living with his abuse for so long, I finally realized that I was not supposed to live like this."

Melanie found a new home for herself and her children. She filed for divorce and eventually began dating again. She had a child with a new boyfriend, but a year and a half later he was dead, murdered by his best friend.

"I began to feel as though I couldn't go on any more. It felt like it was just one bad thing happening after the next. I started using drugs and alcohol to numb my pain, but it didn't work. I asked my sister to take me to a church. She laughed at me because I was a drug addict and everything else, but she did take me and I liked it. I started attending a church where they took really good care of single moms with children. I was still on drugs and alcohol for about a year until I woke up and said to the Lord, 'Hey, I want to believe in you; I want to trust you and rely on you. I want to get some kind of life.' From that day forward I didn't do any more drugs or alcohol.

"The day I turned to God for help was a turning point for me. I wish it could be that I just said, 'Oh, I'm just going to change now,' but it didn't happen that way for me. I started building my self-esteem even more. I started realizing that you can make the right choices and you don't have to accept anything and everything that has been told to you. You can walk a straight path. So I started working with kids in my community. Working with them really gave me a lot more hope. These kids were coming in droves because they said, 'You've been through so much and look where you are today.' "

Melanie's trials were still not over. As she rebuilt her life, news came that her stepfather, the man who had killed her sister and mother and abused her, had died. She found it in her heart to forgive him and gave the eulogy at his funeral. Several years later even more forgiveness would be demanded of her. Her middle son, a U.S. Marine, was killed by a young gang member he had been mentoring.

"You can make the right choices and you don't have to accept anything and everything that has been told to you."

—Melanie Washington

"I went to meet with the boy in prison. I asked him how he could do such a thing to someone who was trying to help him. He didn't have a response. I told him, 'I know that my son loved you and because he loved you, I love you. You have life in prison with no chance of parole. You will never see those streets again, but I want you to have hope in prison. You can be helpful to someone else in prison, to the other young people that I'm talking to. You need to tell them what it's like to murder like that and what's going on in your heart. How do you feel about that? You are going to have to do something with what you did. You just can't sit here and rot away. You have to be able to touch other lives from here. I forgive you. I love you. Today you are my son.

"All he could do was start crying. He couldn't believe me. He asked me, 'Why do you forgive me? Why do you care about what's happening with me? Why do you write and send books and do these things?'

"I said, 'Because I love you. My son loved you, and he must have found something in you that he thought was worthwhile, and that's what I'm looking for in you.' So this young man has been writing letters to kids in prison, and he is doing wonderful in prison and getting his life together. He even graduated college while in prison.

"I want people to understand that we can make it out of situations. We can change our minds and make a choice that is much better for us. We can stop running around feeling sorry for ourselves and pick ourselves up and say, 'No, I'm not going to do this anymore!'"

Melanie lost her mother, sister, boyfriend, and son to violent deaths, all of them killed by repeat offenders who had no support system when they had been released from prison for previous crimes. She wanted to make sure that young people had somewhere to go and someone to guide them after they came out of prison so that they wouldn't repeat the cycle of violence. That passion created MATFA.

"I don't want these kids coming out and hurting anybody else's children, so I'm in there showing them a better way and helping them to get into school and getting them jobs when they get out." The young men get job training and placement, preparation for the work world, educational assistance, scholarships, family counseling, and drug and alcohol rehabilitation within one year of their release. MAFTA also assists crime victims' families.

Melanie Washington is a perfect example of someone who could have chosen to take on a victim mentality but instead decided to use her negative experiences to strengthen her resolve to make a positive difference in the world.

Problem or predicament?

There is simply no avoiding it—storms in life will happen that will threaten to blow you far off course from your destination. Barriers will arise in one form or another. Some will be problems, others will be predicaments. It is important you know the difference between the two and how to deal with each because each requires a different course of action.

A problem is a negative, unexpected event. It can happen by accident through no fault of your own. For instance a tree limb falls on your house during a storm or a business competitor introduces a new product or service that threatens your market share or your career. A problem can also be a mistake you make. You may have said something impulsively out of anger and frustration that you came to regret. Most important realize that every problem has a solution. Face the fact that you made a mistake; apologize when needed and correct the situation as soon as possible. Make amends and be certain that you never make that mistake again.

A predicament, on the other hand, is the result of a behavior pattern that keeps getting you into difficulty. For example alcoholism, out-of-control spending, lying, cheating, procrastination, or other self-destructive behaviors and addictions can lead to predicaments such as the loss of your job, the disintegration of your marriage, bad credit, or poor health. Predicaments have symptoms that mask the core issue. Symptoms can appear as anxiousness, irritability, hostility, restlessness, sleeplessness, the inability to slow down, thoughtlessness, procrastination, inconsideration, depression, or debt. A predicament is the result of habitual behavior that has evolved into unconscious behavior. Because the behavior is habitual as well as unconscious, as time goes on it becomes more difficult to recognize it for what it is.

Predicaments can be addressed and resolved, but not until the underlying cause is identified. A predicament becomes solvable only by recognizing the real issue for what it really is: the barrier standing in the way of a fulfilling and productive life—the best of your life.

Our friend Mary Hunt provides a great example of someone who turned a predicament into an asset. Her predicament started simply enough.

"Within days of my wedding, I suggested to my new husband that we should look into getting a gasoline credit card," she says. "After all, I reasoned, we were now in a different social strata and every real family must be prepared for unforeseen emergencies.

"Wow! Free gas whenever we wanted! No more digging around for loose change to pump gas into the car. Never again would I have to be concerned with mundane issues like the price of gas. By the time the babies came along, however, the gasoline company had canceled the first credit card. I had been late with payments quite a few times and had even missed some along the way. Not to worry though. In addition to a nice assortment of gasoline cards, I had added cards from every department store in Southern California."

The credit cards grew into a proliferation of plastic that would rival a toy factory. And unlike the gasoline companies, the credit card companies didn't require full payment each month. For Mary that was equivalent to pouring gasoline on a fire.

"I had a checkbook too. Often I would neglect to record checks I wrote. It was safer that way because my husband couldn't track my spending. His unobservant temperament became my ally. I could all but redecorate the entire house and he wouldn't notice. I worked under the philosophy that somehow by the time the check was ready to clear, I would magically come up with funds that I could sneak into the bank! Even though that never happened, I still would write checks, often with reckless abandon."

Mary eventually realized that she had a predicament. What was it that she was not seeing? What was it that she didn't want to see?

"I was attempting to go back and fix my own childhood by giving my children all the clothes, toys, and attention I missed as a child. I was trying to fill a void by giving gifts that were bigger and better than the recipient could believe. I was living out the only agenda I knew: External appearances were all that was important when I was growing up. Anything going on inside that conflicted with a perfect facade was ignored, denied, and put aside."

Mary pinpointed the core issue: She was buying things as false security and psychological compensation for childhood losses. She ultimately realized that her so-called solutions to security were in fact catalysts for crisis. Mary had to admit the painful but necessary truth that her behavior was mortgaging her family's future. It was the beginning of a new way of life that took 13 years and paying off more than $100,000 in unsecured debt plus penalties and interest to correct. It was one step at a time, all with the realization that her self-worth is not dependent upon her net worth—what she could buy.

While attending one of Mick's leadership presentations, Mary felt encouraged enough to start an organization called Cheapskate Monthly (now called Debt-Proof Living). She took her well-earned credo public: "Bringing dignity to the art of living below your means." Her successful and beneficial organization is now impacting millions of people, helping them to distinguish between their problems and their predicaments. Her honest message met with overwhelming success and has resulted in the release of her 14th book, *Live Your Life for Half the Price*. Today her website attracts more than 12 million hits a month and features Mary's constant themes of financial responsibility, empowerment, and hope.

Motivation to change

In reality most people want to change. Five years from now your life won't be exactly as it is today. You wouldn't want it to be. Most likely you're probably hoping that your life and lifestyle have improved. Even with the best of intentions, however, people rarely accomplish meaningful change unless they experience a crisis. It's a sense of urgency—real or imagined—that motivates most people to evaluate their lives, make long overdue changes, or break away from their normal routines.

Like Cholene Espinoza, the airline pilot described in Chapter 1, people often need a crisis point to force them to ask crucial questions in their lives. It happens with the person diagnosed with lung cancer who finally gives up smoking or with the alcoholic in a drunk-driving accident who finally joins AA. But no one needs to wait for a crisis. You don't have to experience everything firsthand to learn. You don't have to spend your way into bankruptcy to learn the dangers of credit-card-driven shopping. The tragedy of waiting for a crisis is that you don't see the light until you feel the heat. But when you look for the light, the insight arrives before the heat comes. Prevention is the best solution. Start saving for retirement when you're younger and your older years will go by more smoothly. Have health checkups on a regular basis instead of waiting for symptoms to appear. Pack your parachute before you jump—it's difficult to do on the way down!

So what keeps so many people from making changes? They want to change; they know a change would lead to a better life. What holds them back? The most powerful enemy of change is fear. Did you know there are more than 2,000 classified fears in the medical encyclopedia? Many are well-known, but some you've never heard of. For instance epistemophobia is fear of knowledge. Plutophobia is fear of wealth. There is even a fear of books: bibliophobia. The phobia that is most likely to get in the way of all your efforts to better your behavior and transform bad habits is tropophobia—the fear of change.

We all harbor at least a little fear that change is the death of a part of ourselves. When we think about change, the first thought that hits us at an emotional level is usually not what we are going to gain but what we will have to give up.

> ## The most powerful enemy of change is fear.

Leaving the familiar can be momentarily numbing or scary. Some people can have a sudden, unexpected feeling of loss even at the same time they experience a happy event, like the day they get married. Even though the bride and groom have planned their special day, love each other, and want to spend the rest of their lives together, at the same time they are saying goodbye to their past, to the protection of their parents, and to the independence of single life. And yet because the bride and groom have spent considerable time deciding who they are and what they want, they can push their fears aside and move forward.

Moving beyond that first thought of "what I'm giving up" is what's important; then you can focus on the advantages of what will be.

The impostor syndrome

Tropophobia can take another form, giving fear another voice to hold people back from constructive change. It's the fear that they don't deserve something better, that they are unqualified. Despite the opinion of others, despite the truth of the situation, they feel like frauds, like impostors. That's fear speaking, and when the impostor syndrome takes over, it can have unfortunate consequences.

Anyone can be hijacked by the impostor syndrome. It's an all-too familiar story. The more you achieve, the louder an inner voice whispers, sometimes screams, "Impostor! You don't deserve this!" The impostor syndrome affects your ability to internalize past and current successes. No matter the successes or accomplishments, a person can experience feelings of inadequacy. People who feel like impostors fear the responsibility and visibility that come with success. This is accompanied by a fear of failure, a fear of being "found out." They say to themselves: "I can give the impression that I am more competent than I really am," or "I'm afraid that others will discover I'm not qualified for this position," or "My classmates or coworkers are going to find out I don't really belong here," or "I don't deserve this great relationship."

> Many of us spend too much time worrying about how we measure up to ideals we've created in our minds.

Many hardworking people who are promoted to a new position with a higher salary, bonus, and other perks begin doubting themselves. Often with the new position or assignment they feel somewhere deep inside that they don't really deserve or are not qualified for that great new job. They worry that the new job they have been hoping for and working so hard for will be too much for them. They begin to fear that they're not ready for the new responsibilities and the expectations of others. They suddenly grow concerned about the changes they need to make.

The impostor fear does not discriminate—it's an equal opportunity syndrome. It's as true of CEOs as it is parents or teachers. Their fear is they will be "found out"—even with their widely recognized quantifiable successes.

Mick once spoke at a retreat outside of Philadelphia where he talked about the impostor fear. The 32 men in attendance were all high achievers. The group was made up of PGA champions, NFL stars, a former vice president of the United States, a major sports broadcaster, one of the top estate attorneys in the nation, and other financially and professionally successful people. The discussion of the impostor syndrome hit them at a gut level. All of them—without exception—admitted it had haunted them throughout their careers. Several confessed to hearing an inner voice whisper, "They'd be disappointed if they really knew," "You're only here because of luck or your contacts," or "They're going to discover the phony you are." Yes, they had learned to cope with it. They had learned how to identify it and push it back. They realized it was irrational to think that way. But nonetheless it was something they had to both acknowledge and dismiss on a regular basis.

People with Ph.D.s fear others will discover they are not as smart as others think they are. In our consulting work we often hear someone with a Ph.D. confess, "If others only knew how much I really don't know, they would be highly disappointed in me." Our response is usually, "It's true! You're not as smart as people think you are. Welcome to the human race!" (We both have advanced degrees, and our wives are fond of telling us that we are educated beyond our intelligence!)

The impostor feeling is not limited to education or careers. It extends into all facets of life. Many people spend too much time worrying about how they measure up to ideals they've created in their own minds. They have a fantasy about how they should be or what they think others expect them to be. For example many mothers feel like impostors. They expect some great nurturing instinct to kick in once a child is born that will tell them what the motherly thing to do is in every situation.

When that doesn't happen they begin to think, "I'm not like the other 'perfect' moms all around me." Yet the "perfect" moms they admire are most likely feeling the same way. The mythological mom who flawlessly wins the court case and then drives herself to the hospital to have her baby; who returns to her law office in two weeks; who sends her kids to an Ivy League university and strikes fear in any racquetball player at the Y, male and female alike—that person is at best an alien and at worst an illusion. Any mom who buys into that fantasy is fresh meat for the impostor syndrome.

Supermom meets kryptonite

Lynne Desmond Cage was striving to be just such a superwoman until an illness caused her to reevaluate her preconceived ideas of what it meant to be a good mother and a successful woman. After some life planning sessions with Bob, Lynne decided to leave her corporate job as a human resources executive and begin her own consulting business. In that new role she traveled the globe to meet with clients and give presentations, wrote articles for magazines and newspapers, and worked on a book. She enjoyed being physically active and regularly rode bikes, swam, and attended exercise classes. On top of that she always made it a priority to spend time with her family and be present at her children's games and recitals.

Then one day she started noticing changes to her body. "I started to get severe muscle aches every time I moved my body. I had swollen glands, headaches, pain through my legs and my hands, and it got to a point where I was in bed almost unable to move. I decided it was time to go see a doctor."

After visits to several different doctors, Lynne was diagnosed with a debilitating and incurable disease.

"This has been a tough challenge for me and my family because I can't do the things that I used to do." Lynne has come to realize that although she can't "be there" for her children in the same way she used to be, she can still have a deep and meaningful impact on their lives and she is still a great mom.

"I have been doing a lot of grieving and self-reflection. Most of my self-reflection is 'I can't do that any longer, but what can I do? What do I have control over?' I have control over my mindset and what I think. I am accepting that something is different, and being an overachiever most of my life I have to accept that being superwoman is not a reality. That's a myth I'm no longer falling for.

"My daughter Kelsey said to me the other day, 'Mom, I know it really bothers you that you can't do some of the things that you used to do with us, but really our lives haven't changed that much. Our lives are still really good, and you are always there for us with what is most important. I have to help out a little more and sometimes I groan about it, but you are still there.' That was such a great gift that she gave me because I still have a tendency to think about all the things that I can't do and she was trying to say to me, in her wise 15-year-old way, 'Hey, it's OK; you still do a lot for us.'"

Lynne had to find ways to cope with the unexpected, involuntary changes in her life that seemed to hit her blindsided and unprepared. She is learning to accept her new limitations and how they affect her life and is coming to terms with the fact that she can no longer fulfill the same roles she used to. She's not attempting to live up to the impostor syndrome's expectations for what she used to regard as her role as "mother." She's redefined her role and is renewing her life in a way she never expected. She's living the best of her life.

Human beings are designed to be adaptable, flexible, and resilient, physically and emotionally. We handle enormous amounts of variety in our lives and for the most part we survive just fine. But we also need anchors.

When everything is flying off the walls and coming unglued, you need to have something in your life that does not change. There are so many things you can't control, but the one thing you do have control over is being true to yourself. Telling the truth to yourself becomes your greatest ally in living the life you want. It hurts when others lie to you, but it's deadly when you lie to yourself. Nothing blocks the life and future you really desire like a lack of truth. Honesty to self is the underlying foundation of Four-Dimensional Thinking. It is the mortar that holds each dimension to the others. It is the nucleus of the cellular makeup of each dimension.

For Reflection

Think about the following questions before you turn to the next chapter. Review your answers on a quarterly basis and you will see the degree at which you are managing self-leadership and how effectively you have transformed predicaments into problems that you are solving. This is an ongoing process that is part of the journey to the best of your life!

1. How do I demonstrate my values through my behavior?

2. What are my predicaments? What are my problems?

3. Have I ever felt like an impostor? Knowing what I know now, how would I feel and what would I do differently?

4. What is the one question I'm afraid to ask myself?

5. How do I respond to change? Am I reactive, thinking about what I will lose? Or am I proactive, thinking about what I will gain?

Chapter 3

The First Dimension

Who Are You and What Do You Want?

A ship in the harbor is safe, but that's not what ships are built for.

William Shedd

*D*issecting almost anything creates clarity but also poses a danger. Maybe you remember ninth-grade science class, when you were given the assignment of dissecting a frog. The purpose in school was to isolate and study the parts of the frog—muscles, bones, and organs—to learn how they worked together. When you touched a probe to a particular area, an eye would blink or a leg would move. It was an enlightening experience and resulted in a deeper understanding of a frog's makeup. But of course you also discovered that the frog no longer worked. In this chapter and the three chapters that follow, the Four Dimensions are presented one at a time. As the Four-Dimensional model is dissected, you will see how each dimension is integrated with and complements the other three dimensions. As you begin your journey of self-discovery, remember that all four of the dimensions are necessary to plotting the course for the best of your life. All four dimensions are connected to each other. They are interrelated. And it's when you don't realize the relationship, the connections, and how they are interrelated that you end up with some very unhappy frogs.

Your past, present, and future who

Many people say that the subject of who they are and what they want is something they hadn't seriously considered before. Maybe they'd heard the question in one form or another a million times but never seriously thought about it. So now is the time—just as it has always been.

As a child you probably had lots of ideas about what you wanted to do when you grew up, but you were restricted by the boundaries of age, inexperience, lack of education, and parental control. Now that you're an adult and supposedly free to do as you please, do you? Do you share your dreams with your spouse, boss, or friends? Or do you keep them to yourself because you fear what others' reactions might be? Then why were you looking forward to becoming an adult? What made you think that once you grew up, you could become exactly who you are and have what you wanted?

For some, knowing who they are can come at an early age. Rachel Schreiber, a 26-year-old teacher in Northern Virginia, grew up with a learning disability, ADD, yet from the time she was a little girl she dreamed about being a teacher.

"My dad is in the banking business and so we moved six times before I graduated from high school. I always loved being at school—I liked the whole day itself and never wanted to leave. When I came home I'd teach my little sister, who was three years younger. I even made her do homework. I lined my stuffed animals up in my room as if they were students. My first-grade teacher from Atlanta gave me a necklace for a high school graduation present, which I still wear and think of her and her impact on me in my first year of school. My third-grade teacher got me to really love reading. I was diagnosed with ADD in fourth grade. As I grew older it became a struggle for me to sit still. I had to make myself pay attention.

"Different learning skills, such as reading, were tough for me. I would read a few pages, and then I'd have to go back to read them again because my mind would wander. In high school my softball coach, who was also my science teacher, had a conference with my mom and said, 'She's a very smart girl but she is not doing as well as I know she can do.' I started taking medication and immediately my grades went from C's and D's on tests to A's and B's.

"In high school I started thinking more about what I wanted to do. During one spring break our family took a trip to Arizona. We stayed on a reservation, and I got to interact with the school-children. One student told me that she was the sixth of seven kids. At night she had to pick her dad up at the bar on the corner and drive him home. I thought, 'You are 7 years old—how are you doing this?' She came home at night and cooked dinner for the family because her mom would not always come home. I remember looking at her the day before I left and said to her, 'You could become the president of the United States, the first woman president.' She was in second grade and was probably the smartest girl in the class—the top reader, the top math student. I continued, 'Don't let anybody tell you that you can't do something, because you can do anything.' It was then I decided that I wanted to teach, especially kids with a troubled past or a troubled present.

"My passion for teaching kept growing. I attended Elon University in North Carolina because it has an outstanding teaching program. I traveled to Australia and Europe and also developed a passion for teaching English as a second language. I loved the feeling of teaching little kids something that they have never heard before."

Rachel now teaches in a public elementary school that has more than a thousand children. "Sixty percent of my students are Indian, Middle Eastern, and Asian. So for many of the children I get to teach English as a second language. I feel like I have mini-epiphanies every day because I am learning so much from my kids. Every day I have a story that reaffirms my choice to teach.

"For example, I had a student, Danny, who we eventually figured out was austistic. Danny had been homeschooled in kindergarten, and his parents said he had never really been around kids. It was Danny's first day of school and my first day of teaching, so neither of us had done this before. I had to figure out how to handle him, and he had to figure out how to handle himself. I had to take everything I learned in school and college and readjust my teaching to accommodate his needs. I came home every day very tired, and some days I just cried. But I knew this was what I wanted to do.

"I could have walked into my principal's office and said, 'I don't understand how to teach this little boy and all these other children with other disabilities.' Somehow I knew I had to stay with it and help each and every one of them. I even did some research and wrote a book about working with the children at my school.

"On the last day of class, Danny gave me a high five, and then I knew that I had finally gotten through. It brought tears to my eyes. I was proud to feel like I made a difference in his life.

"There are so many people out there who are not enjoying what they are doing. I know I can't like every minute of teaching, but sometimes I'm feeling frustrated, and a little kid will look up and say something that will make me laugh. Or another will say, 'Oh, I get it!' Their little lightbulbs go on, and I just love that! I love knowing what I want to do."

What's really important?

Our society exerts constant pressure to be successful, which is why defining what success means to you is vital to your future. If you don't define success in your life, others will define it for you. You may find yourself climbing some ladder, only to discover that once you get to the top, it's leaning against the wrong wall.

Lasting success depends on having your personal and professional goals in alignment with your values. For example, if you say what you value most in your life is your family, yet you are so focused on work that you constantly miss opportunities to spend quality time with them, you're out of alignment. You're not being honest with yourself. Living your values would mean changing your behavior to spend time with your family. When you know what your values are and make choices and decisions based on these values, you feel more satisfied. Whether you always accomplish what you want in the short run, knowing you are on the journey to your destination softens the bumps. Once you know where to aim, you're more likely to hit your target.

Patrick Lencioni is the founder and president of The Table Group, a San Francisco Bay Area management consulting firm specializing in executive team development and organizational effectiveness. Pat, author of best sellers *The Five Temptations of a CEO* and *The Five Dysfunctions of a Team*, applies his core values in his own business when making decisions that have long-term impact on his organization—and on himself. "We've been very blessed with success," he told us. "When demand for our consulting services went way up, we had a decision to make. People were encouraging us to grow, saying, 'You should be hiring more consultants!' 'You should be taking on more work!' 'You should be taking equity in your clients to share in their wealth because you don't know how long this is going to last!'

If you don't define success in your life, others will define it for you.

"I remember asking, 'What am I here for? What is the purpose of this company?' My family and my faith have to be more important than some pursuit of financial- or recognition-related goals. So my truth is that I should pursue those things—faith, family, and impact on people—and make a decision to forgo the lie, which is that money and fame and fortune and recognition will make me happy. That's not going to save my soul, and it's not going to help those around me. I needed to pursue what I know is true, which is family, faith, and impact on others over fame and fortune."

Aim for the sweet spot

In the life-planning workshops and retreats we lead, we help people prepare to answer "Who are you and what do you want?" with an exercise that will help them discover what we call their sweet spot. Do this: On a blank sheet of paper, draw three intersecting circles that overlap in the middle (see the illustration below). Label the first circle Strengths and in it write words that describe your talents, gifts, and abilities. In the second circle, labeled Passions, write the things that you highly value and are passionate about—those things that motivate you. Label the third circle Obligations and write in it the things that you are obligated to do to meet your needs and commitments. They might be fun or they might be hard, but you are doing them. They are things you currently are obliged to do. With some reflection and analysis you might discover some are more necessary than others, and some—with further thought—might not be necessary at all. These could be eliminated, while other things that fit with both your strengths and passions could be added.

The place where these three circles overlap is what we call the sweet spot. When you show up to an activity or a job that you're gifted at, passionate about, and committed to, you're living in your sweet spot. The more these three circles are aligned, the larger your sweet spot grows.

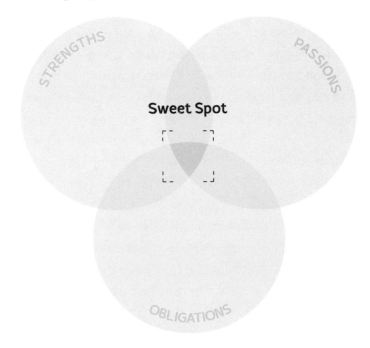

You can't control your strengths and passions; you can only develop them. That takes insight, intention, and discipline. Your obligations, however, are more flexible and can be altered more immediately. They are important for you to control when you have the opportunity. In fact you must take every opportunity to control your obligations, or someone else will. If you don't make these decisions, someone else will. Obligations are an important key to aligning your talents and passions and growing your sweet spot.

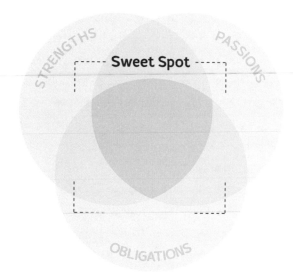

Are you using your strengths—your unique gifts and talents—to their fullest potential? Are you actively pursuing your passions or suppressing them? Do you feel content? Your passions and strengths are the clues to your personal destiny. What you direct your attention to grows stronger in your life—it's the simple law of attraction.

Playing to your strengths

In the 1940s George Reavis, a former assistant superintendent of the Cincinnati Public Schools, wrote a fable that illustrates the importance of playing to your strengths.[1]

Once upon a time the animals decided they must do something heroic to meet the problems of "a new world." So they organized a school.

They adopted an activity curriculum consisting of running, climbing, swimming, and flying. To make it easier to administer the curriculum, all the animals took all the subjects.

The duck was excellent in swimming, in fact better than his instructor, but he made only passing grades in flying and was very poor in running. Since he was slow in running, he had to stay after school and also drop swimming in order to practice running. This was kept up until his webbed feet were badly worn and he was only average in swimming. But average was acceptable in school, so nobody worried about that except the duck.

The rabbit started at the top of the class in running but had a nervous breakdown because of so much makeup work in swimming.

The squirrel was excellent in climbing until he developed frustration in the flying class, where his teacher made him start from the ground up instead of from the treetop down. He also developed a charley horse from overexertion and then got a C in climbing and a D in running.

The eagle was a problem child and was disciplined severely. In the climbing class he beat all the others to the top of the tree but insisted on using his own way to get there. He was eventually expelled for being a troublemaker.

It's easy to be seduced by the promises offered by some people that "You can have it all! You can do it all!" However it's healthier to keep a realistic perspective. As that great philosopher Clint

Eastwood said in the film *Dirty Harry*, "A man's got to know his limitations." You are more effective when you focus on and pursue the things you're skilled at—it's how your brain is wired. You can waste time, money, and energy pursuing unrealistic goals. A woodworker would say that it's much easier to work with the grain than against it.

Our advice: Don't abandon your dreams, but make sure your dreams are ultimately attainable.

Knowing your passions

Strengths don't always match up with what we're passionate about. When you align your talents and passions, they support—even amplify—one another. You are more effective when your strengths complement your passions. When you find the right combination, you develop them both.

Just because it's a personal strength or talent doesn't mean it won't take some discipline. Tiger Woods has both the talent and passion to play golf, yet nobody works harder at the game or spends more hours at the driving range than he does. After 14 hours of hitting balls at the driving range he says, "Each time I hit the ball, it's different."

Dale Carlsen's passion drove him to open the first Sleep Train store in Sacramento, California, and to become the largest retailer of mattresses on the West Coast and one of the top three in the United States. Since he founded the company in 1985, Sleep Train has opened stores up and down the West Coast.

"I started out just as a flunky," he says, "emptying the garbage, answering the phones, and all that kind of stuff. Then the owners of the mattress manufacturing company I worked for took me under their wing, so I started to learn more about their business. I did some computer programming for them, and eventually they offered me a job as a salesman. I went on the road selling Monday, Wednesday, and Friday, while I went to school on Tuesdays and Thursdays. I enjoyed sales, no doubt about it. But then I graduated, and my degree was in real estate finance and insurance. I always thought I wanted to be a commercial real estate broker, so I interviewed with two real estate companies."

Even though both agencies offered Dale jobs, he ultimately decided to continue working for the mattress company. As a sales manager Dale visited all the stores in his district to advise them how to boost their lagging sales. Even though the salespeople seemed enthused by his ideas, they didn't change their methods. He knew that there was a better way to sell mattresses, and that inspired him to start his own company. And in the process of developing his skills, he found his passion.

"Who would think anyone would be passionate about beds? I said it early on and ever since—my passion is about people. It isn't mattresses, it's people—working with people. Initially it was about how people can get a better night's sleep for a better deal. Give them the answers to questions they haven't thought about regarding buying a mattress. Provide buyers customer service, which when I first started in the industry wasn't there. Anybody could tell you, 'The product is on sale,' or give you an 'Isn't it pretty?' type of a pitch. To me we needed to tell the customer why there were hundreds of dollars of difference between different beds. Providing that information was part of my passion, knowing that I was helping someone's mental and physical health."

Dale wanted to become successful in selling real estate, but what emerged along the way was discovering that he was a natural salesperson, he could sell anything he wanted to as long as it filled a need. What he understood that others didn't, given the same circumstances, is that people buy for a reason and that by providing his customers with useful and needed information, he could outsell his competition. When no one wanted to take his suggestions, he took them himself and made his life and the lives of those who work for him something special. Yet does Dale see that about himself? Probably not; instead if you ask him, Dale will say that his favorite part of owning his company is helping his 1,400 employees find their passions too. "What is it that drives them? What excites them? You've got to really believe in what you are doing and believe in what you are trying to accomplish. What drives me now isn't to make more money or to open more stores. My passion is to watch the people I'm fortunate to work with develop and become leaders. I've got kids that started working with me when they were just out of college, and now they are leaders and district managers, experts at motivating their people."

Schedule your values

While your talents and passions are there to be discovered and developed, you can control one area of your life starting this very moment. You can choose what you do with your time.

> If you don't schedule your
> time, others will do so for you.

On the journey for the best of your life, one of the major course corrections you must learn to handle is evaluating how you use your time. This is key to aligning your obligations with your strengths and passions, thus enlarging your sweet spot. It's important to develop your perspective about time. If you don't schedule your time, others will do so for you. Most people let other people set their agendas. To get what you truly want, it is important to develop the habit of scheduling according to your values—scheduling what is really important to you. Make sure your important activities and events are on your schedule before others fill it up with things that are not nearly as important to you. So don't just fill in your calendar with appointments and tasks. Take a step back and look at it as scheduling your values by answering these questions:

What do I want to be?

What do I want to do?

What do I need to learn?

With whom do I need to spend time?

Make your to-don't list

Almost everyone has a to-do list. And it seems that we just keep adding and adding to our schedules. The trouble is that we don't subtract as fast as we add, and that kind of math doesn't work for finite human beings. Ron Heifetz, director of the Center for Public Leadership at Harvard, says, "When you are engaging in any kind of strategy, you are really asking yourself to sift through what you are NOT going to do." So try this: Make yourself a to-don't list and then give yourself permission not to do the items on that list. Focus happens only when you are not spread thin by overobligating your schedule. The things that don't fit must be eliminated. *The secret of concentration is elimination.* People who achieve the most are determined *and* selective. Most people are stuck in races in which other people have entered them. That's why the results are mediocre. Lack of personal satisfaction comes from entering the wrong races—races that don't fit with your strengths and passions. Satisfying achievements come from races you yourself enter. Make sure they are your races and not theirs.

Vicki Halsey is vice president of Applied Learning at the Ken Blanchard Companies. She is a presenter, keynote speaker, consultant, and coach for companies such as Nike, Toyota, Gap Inc., Merrill Lynch, and Wells Fargo. She is also coauthor of *The Hamster Revolution: How to Manage Your Email Before It Manages You*. Before Vicki joined the Ken Blanchard Companies, she worked in the education system.

"I was assistant school principal and all of a sudden I realized, 'I'm killing myself here. What do I love? I love the kids and I love being with the kids.' But I was just running like a madwoman. I made a list of 16 things I was doing that were not my core job. I was running an aspect of the California School Leadership Academy; I was on the state retirement committee; I was president-elect for the administrative group in the school district. At the time I thought I needed to be defined by what I did. I was doing, doing, doing, and I realized that's not how I want to be defined. I want to be defined by who I am. So literally within a 24-hour period, I resigned from 12 of those things."

The amazing part of Vicki's story is not only that she found a way to clear the areas of her life that were cluttering it but also that she added meaning and joy to other people's lives at the same time. She explains: "I didn't just abandon ship. I called different people and said, 'Would you be interested in this?' I found someone else for whom being able to teach a class at the California School Leadership Academy was the greatest gift of her life. Someone else was so excited to now be president-elect. It was a gift to give other people. Now I can do what actually strengthens me, and I feel like I'm doing what may be my greatest work."

Now when Vicki plans her schedule, she plans in advance. "I used to look out one month; now I'm looking six months at a time. How's my schedule? Is there space in it? If some neat opportunity comes up when I can meet someone or do something I've always wanted to do, I have time in my schedule. I make sure that I haven't filled in too much because there are always so many other things to do. It's a continual diagnosis of where I'm at; what I am doing; how much time I have to do this, that, and the other. What do I want to get done? Am I taking time for me?

"I think the better you figure out who you are, the more you turn back and look at your life, your choices, the tragedies, and the joys. And that helps you get clearer on what you want in your future."

It's tough to have clarity with clutter in our lives. When you take time to pull the weeds, fresh ideas have a better chance of growing. Clutter leads to complacency, and complacency chokes out truth. Over the long haul what will kill you is complacency. It's much worse than a crisis because a crisis gets your attention immediately. Complacency lulls you into a sleep. Like the proverbial frog in the kettle, you don't notice that the water is slowly growing hotter and hotter until you're cooked. One year flows into two and then ten. Like a poor student whom the teacher reluctantly promotes to the next grade, you move on but not up. Ask the complacent employee, "How long have you been a manager?" He'll say, "Ten years." In reality he's been a manager one year, repeated ten times. He's had no growth, learning, or progress—in the same place and doing the same thing over and over. That's complacency choking out a life.

20 will get you 80

More than 100 years ago, the Italian economist Vilfredo Pareto brought to light a principle that helps everyone achieve more with less effort. It's been referred to as Pareto's Law, The Law of Substitution, The Law of the Vital Few, the Principle of Least

Effort, and what is perhaps its best-known name: the 80/20 Principle. It simply states that 80 percent of your productivity is brought about by 20 percent of your effort. The percentages may change depending on what you're doing—the formula shows the imbalance between the efforts you apply and the effects you obtain, the difference between what you do and what you get out of it. Very little effort can result in the majority of the results or rewards you want. To put it another way, most of your efforts in achieving what you want are irrelevant to what you truly want or value. That has major personal implications as you discover at a deeper level who you are and what you want, as you will soon see. It is also a great principle to exercise in growing your sweet spot.

What are the very few things that if done well can make the biggest difference in your life?

You've probably heard the saying that "the good can become the enemy of the best." Identifying the percentage of wasted time and effort in your schedule will become a new source of renewal and energy. You'll find yourself in a position to eliminate the good things that are hindering your journey for the best of your life. Using the 80/20 Principle when deciding anything makes you realize that only a few decisions really matter. They don't have to be perfect either. Those that do matter, matter a great deal. What are the very few things that if done well can make the biggest difference in your life?

As you work through the Four Dimensions with the 80/20 Principle in mind, you will discover that much of what you are currently doing is not contributing to the best of your life. As you assess your activities and commitments, you will probably discover an imbalance between your efforts and effects—between what you do and what you get in return. As you work through the Third Dimension—What will you do and how will you do it?—your plans and goals will be more productive by concentrating your efforts on the effective 20 percent of your time and effort. Its easiest application starts with the First Dimension—knowing who you are and what you want.

Without identifying your preferred future—your destination—you can have all the timesaving techniques in the world and be efficient, yet not effective, simply because you are not going in the direction of what you really want. Why be involved in all kinds of activity without accomplishment? A modern lifestyle can appear to pressure you into hyperkinetic activity if you don't consider the results you want. You can be deluged with an overwhelming number of options. Yet once you develop the conscious habit of considering your choices, you effectively manage your time and stay in control of your agenda. You are effective, multiplying your productivity, increasing the quantity and quality of what you do, think, and say by making the choice to be that way from the beginning of your journey. You're happy because you want to be all along the way. That's a "sweet spot" to be in.

The goal is not merely to achieve what you finally want; it's to enjoy every step of the way getting there. It's not about enjoying only the result; it's about enjoying the process and the changes you discover in yourself as you move on. It's not a matter of putting up with drudgery until you eventually grab some gold ring at the end of the ride. As Warren Buffett says, "That would be like saving up sex for old age!"

Balance alone is not a satisfying goal

Balance started as a good concept, but it has become little more than a buzzword today. As an end in itself, it has no real advantage. Some use the term "balance" as an anesthetic to dull the pain of an empty life. It's very possible to live a balanced life with all the parts in place and functioning and yet not have a clue who you really are or what you really want. Until you know what is valuable to you, what does having a balanced life really mean? Most things don't end up being perfectly balanced anyway. Not for long. What things are meaningful to you? They aren't perfectly balanced.

You can have 15,000-square-foot fully-staffed homes in three cities, a jet plane, a garage full of luxury cars, the most fashionable clothing; you can look like you're on top of the world—yet if you don't have values, you might as well be on top of the world aboard the *Titanic*. Is that who you are and is that having what you want?

As business researcher and consultant W. Edwards Deming once said, most people's lives are like the food in his refrigerator— not quite good enough to eat but not quite bad enough to throw out either. It's a life of mediocrity, and as they near the end of it, they find out that they're not happy with what they have. A commitment to the truth of who you are and what you want, on the other hand, is a commitment to bettering your life. Knowing that is the 20 percent that will make the biggest difference in how you feel about yourself and the life you lead.

For Reflection

Assess your strengths, passions, and obligations in depth using the following exercises. Your answers are for you alone. There's no need to be self-conscious. Self-consciousness is how you view other people looking at you. Self-awareness is knowing yourself at a deep level. To take charge be self-aware.

Look over all of the questions before you begin. Write your answers in your notebook or on your computer and date them. Review your answers a month from today.

My Strengths Assessment

1. What have I done in the past that gave me a sense of satisfaction?
2. What are three things I do well?
3. What are my strengths? How do I use them?
4. What do others say are my strengths?

My Passions Assessment

A wise person once said, "While you're thinking think big! You can always act small later." There is always the danger of immediately putting limitations on your thinking.

Be realistic but also recognize that in an attempt to be practical, you may often end up playing it safe and developing imagination gridlock.

1. List things I would like to do well. List experiences I would like to have. What do I want to start doing right now?
2. What are five nonnegotiable values in my life? What things, events, or activities make me feel fully alive?
3. What have I let slide? Why? What can I do now to reverse that?
4. What would be my "perfect day" at work? At home?

5. What would I do if I were guaranteed success in each of the various areas of life?

6. Write a paragraph describing your life if you were using all your talents and abilities.

My Obligations Assessment

Most people use their schedules to let other people set their agendas. They are adapting their schedules to meet other people's expectations. After reading this chapter you know how to make your schedule reflect your own agenda and what's important to you. Reflect on and answer the questions that follow. Your most powerful insights will be generated through reflection without any need for additional information. Your brain already has more information than you can imagine, and reflecting will bring your best ideas to the surface. This kind of thinking is unconventional simply because most people don't take the time to do it.

1. What is on my schedule that doesn't need to be there? What things can be abandoned or at least cut back? What obligations am I creating for six months from now that I will regret then?

2. List some things I've always wanted to do. Are any of these reflected on my schedule? Weekly? Monthly? Yearly?

3. What am I doing that I don't enjoy doing? What am I doing that I love to do?

4. What is the 20 percent of my effort that produces 80 percent of the results I want to accomplish?

5. What are the things other people want me to do? What are the things that I want to do?

6. What are some things I would like to do that fall under the category of "now or never"?

Chapter 4

The Second Dimension

Where Are You and Why Are You There?

We can easily forgive a child who is afraid of the dark; the real tragedy of life is when adults are afraid of the light.

Plato

Y ou're at a shopping mall to meet a friend for lunch at a place you've never been. You make your way through the labyrinth parking area and realize it's not going to be easy to locate the restaurant. The mall has hundreds of stores and a dozen corridors that all look alike. You find a directory and eventually spot the name. You realize you're still directionally challenged until you see that familiar dot that says, "You Are Here." You are relieved because now you know it'll be a lot easier to get to where you want with the perspective of where you are. Now plotting your course to the restaurant seems easy.

Where you are and why it matters

Knowing your current location is essential to reaching your desired destination. If you try to download driving directions for a trip, the map service can't respond until you enter a starting point. Before you start your journey to the best of your life, you need a reference point. It's easier to make decisions about your future once you know how your past and present connect to it. Like when you're looking at the directory map at the mall, you need some context. You need a larger picture so you can see where you are in relation to where you want to go. Context provides perspective. It helps show you the direction and how far you have to go. It is an indispensable part of Four-Dimensional Thinking because it leads to the next important part of your journey: choices and decisions.

Throughout your life you have made low-impact choices and high-impact decisions every day, and the cumulative result is where you are right now. You make your choices and decisions and they make you. In assessing where you are and why you are there, you become aware of decisions you regret and wish you could do over and the ones that gave you great results that bear repeating. Some have been productive and others have been counterproductive. First assess where you are and then examine the decision process that brought you there. Making a poor choice or decision is not the problem as much as not recognizing the connection between your current state and the choices and decisions that led you to where you are.

What were some of those choices? What were those decisions? In retrospect which were the most significant? Did they serve you well or poorly? Which ones would you repeat?

Interrogate reality

There's a technical term to describe the state of not knowing how you have traveled to where you are: "stuckness." To quote author and leader Edwin Louis Cole, "You don't drown by falling in the water; you drown by staying there."

For many individuals decisions and choices tend to be un-conscious. They feel like life happens to them. They don't see themselves as the architects of their own lives. Such a reactionary lifestyle can drain anyone of a sense of personal power, control, or confidence. Eventually it will affect his or her emotional and physical well-being.

Conversely those who take the time to stop and reflect find it easier to direct their choices and decisions toward the life they want. They ask themselves questions—hard questions. And they give themselves honest answers. They interrogate reality.

Those who interrogate reality gain 20/20 clarity on the what and why of where they are. They avoid becoming stuck in their lives. The happiest people are far from perfect or without errant choices but are that way because they take full responsibility for where they are and for creating their own lives.

The reflection in the mirror

One major reason why so many don't interrogate their reality is be-cause they've never learned how to stop and reflect. Some fear re-flection, while others allow their busyness to bypass the reflective process because deep emotions are connected with the past. Emo-tions can wipe out a false sense of control, and for some believing they are in complete control of their lives is important. They assume interrogating their reality will be a very painful process.

Modern culture encourages—even rewards—hyperkinetic activity. In that kind of environment, reflection is more essential than ever. Successful people, however, take the time to reflect. There is no real learning process, sense of discovery, or insight without reflection.

The word "reflect" in Latin means "to refold." When you look in the mirror the image goes in, refolds, and reflects. Personal growth comes when you know how to use your mind's mirror. You do that by slowing down and pausing long enough to learn the truth about your life. Take a circumstance or event—a happening—and quietly look inward to reflect on it for as long as it takes, and eventually you will understand something new about the incident that you've never had before. It's your epiphany—an exciting new insight. It's an exhilarating moment.

Tony Batts, chief of police for Long Beach, California's fifth-largest city, had just such a moment. In his job he is used to thinking on his feet and acting in the moment. Chief Batts holds a doctorate in public administration and has received numerous awards and commendations at the local, state, and national levels for heroism, crime reduction, and innovative programs. He is responsible for a staff of 1,500 people in a city with 500,000 residents. In addition he is the first African-American city manager of Long Beach, a position he held in the interim while still performing his duties as chief of police. But it took an experience outside his usual routine to prompt him to see clearly what was driving him and what he really wanted.

"I was in a program called Leadership Long Beach. Part of the program was a ropes course with about 40 to 60 people in the class. Looking the course over I thought, 'These rope exercises aren't a big deal. It's really a waste of time for me, but I'll do it because I'm here to participate.' They had different trust-related activities, including one where people were asked to fall back and have other people catch them. It was eye-opening for me that so many participants were so scared of falling back and not trusting that the other people would catch them. Some just broke down and cried. So I thought this course would be a breeze because having trust is something I do every day in my job. When you're driving in a 100-mile-per-hour car chase, things are moving so fast you've got to count on your fellow officer to tell you what's coming on your right side.

"The course had another event where we had to climb to the top of a pole, which looked higher than a normal phone pole, and at the top of the pole was a disk that we were to stand on. We wore a safety harness and tether. The object was to climb the pole, stand on top of the disk, spin yourself around, and jump down onto the landing mat below. All my teammates went up; some made it and some didn't. My turn came up and the guy in charge, knowing I was the chief, said, 'We're going to make a slight change and push the mat out a little farther for you.'

"I said, 'Push it even farther out. I like a challenge!'

"He said, 'OK!'

"I don't like heights much, but I went up anyway. All along the climb I was fighting my fear of heights, yet I went all the way up. I stood at the top and turned around, but to prepare to jump I had to put one foot behind the other. As I put one foot behind me, I fell off. They lowered me down. When I got to the ground, the guy in charge said, 'Good job, Tony.'

"I said, 'Not a good job. I'm going back up there.'

"He said, 'You can't go back up there.'

"And I said, 'Yes, I am. I'm going back up there and I will

continue to go back up there until I'm successful at what I'm slated to do here.'

"He called the group in and said, 'Tony wants to go back up. What do you think?'

"Another person said, 'Well I didn't get to go again—why should he get to go? Let's give him a group hug and show him we love him!'

"Everybody came in and gave me a hug, and I really wanted to say, 'I don't need a hug from you people!' They didn't notice my resistance and continued on to the next ropes course. I stood there and actually got angry. I said to myself, 'I'm going back up there anyway. I'm not leaving here until I do that right.' I stopped for a second to reflect and thought, 'This really means nothing and for some reason I've made it into an achievement that I have to complete. What's more important are those people who were standing here and saying, "We support you whether you made it or not—it doesn't matter."' That was an epiphany for me because all my life I've focused on achievement as being the reason people would love, respect, or be there for me. For me that was a big moment. I felt a shift happen inside me. From that moment on I started to pay attention to the people in my life, the people who make the most difference to me. Not only my mom and my dad or my children but the other people I love and care about. I started to put more balance in my life and made sure that I started putting my children first in my activities—not the job, not the achievement! That's when I began to do little things like stopping work in the middle of the day to attend a PTA meeting or an event at my kids' school. Those are the kind of things that suddenly became most important in my life. They became my top priority. I'm moving toward doing more with the people I love and with my family."

Reflection is different from introspection. Introspection is simply looking in. Stopping there limits your perspective or even diffuses it. It can lead some people to pessimism and even depression. Reflection is looking in so you can look out with a broader, bigger, and more accurate perspective. Without reflection life becomes happenstance; you run from day to day gaining no real insights. Happenings do not automatically become experiences. This is why so many people can read self-help books and hear motivational speeches without changing anything about themselves. Asking "Where am I and why am I here?" initiates a reflective process. It gives you context. It shows you the red "You Are Here" dot on the map. Self-help is initiated in self-reflection, which leads you from where you are to where you want to go.

The truth of your circumstances

Fred Haise was the lunar module pilot aboard *Apollo 13*, scheduled for a 10-day mission for the first landing in the hilly, upland Fra Mauro region of the moon. The original flight plan, however, was dramatically modified en route to the moon when the service module cryogenic oxygen system exploded 55 hours into the flight. Haise and fellow crewmen James Lovell, spacecraft commander, and John Swigert, command module pilot, working closely with the NASA ground controllers, converted their lunar module, *Aquarius*, into an effective lifeboat to bring them 200,000 miles back to Earth safely.

At the core of their survival plan was a question: Where are we and why are we there? Answering that led to a series of operations that conserved both electrical power and water in sufficient supply to ensure their safety and survival in space and their return to Earth.

"In my line of work, the results can be very dramatic if you've not faced up to reality. There are problems on every flight. This one happened to be fairly major."

> ## "Being successful in life means being honest with both who and where you are." —Fred Haise

According to Haise, this experience is similar to life in general. "Being successful in life means being honest with both who and where you are," he says. "You have to be truthful with yourself to understand your circumstances and the direction you are going. As an astronaut test pilot, you have to be honest with yourself in judging the risk and dealing with the planning, situations, and contingencies for emergencies that occur. It has to be a way of life if you want to be successful, both as a person and as a professional."

Closing the integrity gap

Often there's a gap between what people believe and how they behave—it's called the integrity gap. The word "integrity" comes from a Latin root word that means "entire." It carries the idea of being whole or complete. Like all the areas of your life, integrity involves growth. The integrity gap narrows as you become more in sync with what you say you believe and how you behave. Your relationships, emotional well-being, and health are all affected by your integrity or lack thereof. Your body keeps score of how closely your values and your behaviors align. Research shows that one's level of integrity strengthens or weakens the immune system. The more dissonance there is between your values and behavior, the more stress you experience, which weakens your immune system. The more alignment, the less stress and the healthier your system. Knowing where you are and why you are there helps to close the gap.

Growing in integrity means becoming an authentic person. You are the author of your life, you are authentic. You are not merely the shadow of what you could be. The shadow self is not what you were meant to be.

How do you get rid of a shadow? By putting some light on it—illuminate it. Surgeons never do surgery in the dark. Not every detail is pleasant, but illuminated surgical rooms are essential for a successful operation. Authentic living is a life without shadows. Many pundits think intimacy occurs in the dark. In reality it occurs in the light—having no secrets, withholding nothing, being totally honest with where you are and why you are there is true intimacy. When you close any gap in your integrity, you are taking strong preventive measures to eliminate future problems, invigorate your health, and promote your growth. Knowing where you are and why you are there lights up your life.

Integrity impacts our relationships

We've all seen and way too many of us have experienced the terrible toll that dishonesty exacts on even our most important and cherished relationships. Being out of tune with yourself leads to discord and dysfunction. There is no harmony. The result is visible, and it has a dramatic impact on our lives.

In business the term "organizational alignment" describes when employee actions match the values of the organization. But there's also personal alignment: making sure that your life actions are aligned with your values. There is a direct connection with who you say you are inside and what you're actually doing on the outside. To achieve alignment you're going to need a clear vision for your own life.

Emotional and intellectual attunement

In addition to alignment there's something called attunement that many recognize as passion for being, doing, and living. Attunement is the source of your energy and vitality—if you don't have it you're like a car running smoothly, headed in the right direction, but running out of fuel. In *Primal Leadership: Realizing the Power of Emotional Intelligence*, coauthor Daniel Goleman puts it this way: "Attunement is alignment with the kind of resonance that moves people emotionally as well as intellectually." Attunement arouses passion for vision, a clear picture of the future. When attunement takes hold in relationships, people feel the heat of collective excitement. Enthusiasm in the relationship builds from that point. A shared vision tunes people to a higher calling in their collective lives. It builds resonance—relational harmony. It increases people's capacity to act collectively and enthusiastically.[1]

Jane Roeder today serves as managing director for the Ukleja Center for Ethical Leadership at California State University, Long Beach, an organization that focuses on development of ethical leaders through education and educational programs through community outreach. In addition to developing programs for students, the center works with companies, educational institutions, and nonprofit organizations to advance the practice of ethical leadership at every organizational level. To get to where she is today, though, Jane dealt with alignment in her personal and professional life.

"Growing up I was taught that thinking of myself was selfish, and I learned to put others above myself. As a result it was hard for me to know who I was because I was never concerned about myself. I was focused on others all the time. This is still an issue for me, as I'm sure it is for many women.

"My family and my friends are most important to me. But right near the top of my list is my work. When I have a work life that is aligned with my personal values and what I bring to the world, then everything clicks. That's who I am! I'm particularly appreciative of where I am now because I've come through experiences that haven't always been good. During some of my past personal and professional relationships, there have been times when I've found that those relationships were not based on truth. I was afraid of change and any emotion around moving forward into the unknown.

"In these instances the first symptom is a signal from my gut. A lot of times in the past, however, I ignored this signal because I was too afraid of what would happen next. I tended to see the potential in people and in situations, so I stayed in a situation longer than what was healthy for anyone, especially myself. I missed the reality of my painful present by envisioning a more hopeful or happier future. I only made changes when the discord became so painful I couldn't ignore it."

Jane was teaching third grade when she saw that the executive director of a leadership organization was stepping down. She was immediately interested in the job.

"I was hired as interim director for Leadership Long Beach and then moved on to be director. I was there for seven years. I decided to be counseled by a life coach, who said to me, 'So, Jane, let's talk about your next steps.'

"I said, 'Next steps? I love what I'm doing here.'

"He came back saying, 'Well, that's exactly the time. You want to talk about taking the next step when you are at the top of your game so you can move on to the next level.'

"I didn't even want to have the conversation because I was happy with what I was doing. I loved it." Despite the fact that she felt she had a job she loved, Jane again started sensing something wasn't quite right. "I started having those little churning feelings in my gut telling me, 'Maybe I do need to look at this,' but I still didn't want to look at it because I didn't want to let go. I didn't want any more change, but there were other things I couldn't ignore. During my seventh year there, my son Sean was in his first year of high school. He was failing four subjects. I was working around the clock and was never at home. I looked at what I professed to be my priorities, my values in terms of family coming first and being true to who I am. I thought, 'I'm out of integrity. I say that my family is first, but I'm putting my job first.' I wasn't living my values.

"There were some other things going on and signals from the organization that maybe I was not quite as in alignment with the organization as I thought. So once I recognized that my values were out of alignment, I decided to leave. It was a leap of faith for me because I had no other job lined up, and here I was a single mother supporting two children. Probably not the wisest thing to do, but it ended up being the best thing.

"I gave myself the gift of four months on personal sabbatical where I really focused and reflected on my purpose, my vision, my values, and my gifts. I asked myself, 'What do I want to do next?' I knew that to do a job search through an Internet site, I'd have to have some key words to define who I was. I did some personal assessment because I knew those words were going to be critical. After my personal retreat the four words that I came up with were leadership, education, nonprofit, and spirituality. Now I have all four of those things at my new job at the Center for Ethical Leadership, located four minutes from my house, and now I can be home if Sean needs me."

At the Center for Ethical Leadership, Jane found a place that not only aligned with her values but also gave her the sense of attunement for which she was searching. At the core of alignment and attunement is integrity. Without integrity the group system breaks down because integrity is based on a commitment to truth. Integrity is about being truthful with yourself, which leads to alignment of your behavior with what you say you believe. The result is high performance, both in individual lives and collectively. Think of it as a formula:

$$T(A1+A2) = HP$$

Truth times Alignment plus Attunement equals High Performance

Deep down inside we all want to trust others and to be trusted ourselves—but often it doesn't feel safe. How do you help other people in your life become truthful? And stay that way? It all begins as with everything in your life—with you. When you are truthful others see your vulnerability and it encourages them also to be truthful. Somebody has to take the lead to start the positive cycle, so why not you? People will see that you are vulnerable yet are willing to take the lead: When they feel it's safe for them, they'll want to do the same. You can imagine how much easier it will be for Jane's son Sean to make better decisions about his life after seeing the great example his mother gave him about believing in and staying true to yourself. Helping individuals and groups around you attain attunement will help them grow and help you stay true to yourself.

The lasting value of integrity

Peter Klein is former senior vice president of the Gillette Company. He is responsible for corporate strategy, business planning, business development, and global marketing resources. Previously he was executive vice president at Nabisco, Inc. According to Peter, integrity is important in every aspect of a person's life—from business to family to personal relationships. Understanding what is right and what is wrong is something that anyone should be able to clearly discern. "Integrity is extremely important in my life. My moral compass is clearly aimed: Something is either right or wrong. A commitment to the truth will help me grow in keeping my beliefs and my behavior aligned."

Peter once had an experience that shows how a momentary lapse in integrity can have long-term repercussions on relationships. "Back in my Marketing Corporation of America days, one of my clients was a very large, privately held toiletries and household products business. I was working with the head of strategic planning and external development, who reported directly to the president and CEO. We had done several projects successfully and were asked to assist with an acquisition. Our client made a nonbinding bid and got into the final round. The company came back to us and asked if we could work with them on the final bid. We developed another proposal, and they agreed and signed it.

"Halfway through the project, however, they decided to back out of the auction because the price was getting too high. So I prepared to close out the project right away and bill our fees in proportion to our progress—68 percent—per the signed proposal.

"Our client called and said, 'Can you come down tomorrow so we can talk about the next project?' I said, 'Sure.' We met in his office, along with his CFO. But instead of a discussion about a new project, these guys worked on me for two hours to reduce my company's fees. They wanted to pay 15 or 20 percent of the eight-week fee, not the 68 percent we were due. I explained how the consulting business worked, how we get paid for putting in our time and making our deliverables, and reminded them how they had voluntarily signed the agreement.

"They went on as if that didn't mean anything. They said they wanted to continue to work with my company in the future and I should seriously reconsider our position. I said the best I could do was 65 percent. They weren't happy, but they eventually paid it. That was the last I heard from them.

"Six years later I received a call from the guy who tried to stiff my organization. He said he was being released by his parent company and wanted to know if I could help him find a job. It was as if the earlier example of his complete lack of integrity never happened. I declined, of course, but it made me think: Even if you have no moral compass whatsoever, with the world getting smaller every day, doesn't it make great sense to have integrity? We should all nurture and develop our integrity on a daily basis. Just think of the ways I could have helped this guy out when he needed it. Your integrity is something that follows you around your career, just like your resume. "

Lessons from the carnival

As children both of us authors loved going to the carnival. The fun house was particularly exciting. We would run through the maze of mirrors, not knowing which way to turn. We would leave with little knots on our heads and bruises on our knees from running down what we thought was a hallway only to run into an immovable glass wall. On the way out, the walls of the tiny lobby were lined with wildly curved mirrors with distorted images of the real us. The mirrors made us look tall and skinny or short and fat. Our faces looked warped: big ears, bulging eyes, large nose, fat cheeks. We laughed and laughed because we knew what we saw was distorted—we knew it was not the real us, not the authentic us.

You have an internal mirror that reflects how you see yourself. What you see determines your behavior—often subconsciously.

And when that image is distorted, it's not funny. Who you really are and what you really want can become minimized or exaggerated by what you believe about yourself. Without some honest self-reflection, you expend a lot of energy trying to find the right image to project to others. It's not about being perfect. It's about being honest. And when you find and hold an accurate image of yourself, that's when a sense of well-being and authenticity begins to well up inside. This is why knowing where you are and why you are there is so important in getting a more accurate picture of yourself.

> It's not about being perfect.
> It's about being honest.

Jonathan W., who is now a successful executive search consultant, shared the story about his path to acknowledging and accepting himself for who he is—without distortion—and what he did with that knowledge.

"I hit the wall on February 29. That was the day I said to myself, 'Kill me or fix me, I really don't care which. Just make this stop.' Had someone suggested that I put a gun in my mouth and pull the trigger, I probably would have. My good friend who oddly enough was a drinking buddy suggested I look at an inpatient alcohol treatment facility. After he described it I said, 'Great, let's go do that. And let's do it quickly before I change my mind.' Within three hours I was in a 12-step inpatient treatment facility where I stayed for 28 days.

"Fundamentally what I learned was that alcohol was not the problem; I'm the problem. The alcohol was a means to numb the pain, which came as a result of my inability to know how to deal with life in any aspect: business, personal, or family. The people at the center also taught me something that for me seemed like an unnatural act: Think of others before you think of yourself.

"In reality I had stopped maturing emotionally when I started drinking alcohol, so I was an emotional 14-year-old in a 31-year-old body. I had a lot of maturing to do. That's when I was able to begin to think about things like 'What do I really want?' It could only have happened, though, after I stopped the pain, learned to live in my own skin, and recovered physically and emotionally enough to be able to think about life's big essay question: 'What do I want?'

"When we were kids taking tests in school, everybody wanted the true/false, multiple-choice tests because they were easier. With an essay question we had to actually think. I had never really been forced to answer the essay question 'What do I really want to do?' I'd never been pushed to ask myself that. I was unprepared to answer it.

"You can tell me and extol all the virtues and benefits of making a change in behavior, but I'll wallow in my own junk until it's too painful, or until I see there is such a huge benefit in making a change that I'll be compelled to actually change my behavior. I can't speak for others, but that's what happened for me."

Part of Jonathan's essay answer was to find a career that would be true to his values and his character. "My career had to be taken in the context of my business, personal, family, spiritual, and community life and in the other vital components in my life. One of the things that was important to me was that whatever I did, it had to be of value to people. Ideally it had to make the situation better than it was, and there had to be ample reward. I realized there are different kinds of rewards, but I had become accustomed to a lifestyle that required certain financial rewards. And I was looking for a lifestyle conducive to raising a family, which was something I was sure that I would want soon."

Jonathan considered several different career paths: teaching, acting, serving as a litigator. None seemed to match his authentic self. "Until this point I had been doing something different every 12 to 18 months, running different companies. I was either the sales or marketing officer, president, or chief executive officer. Then because it wasn't satisfying, I'd move on to something else. The only criterion I used at that time: How much does that pay? By this time, however, I had finally reached the point where I was looking for what I really wanted. I still hadn't answered the essay question, but I had identified what my criteria were.

"I was being interviewed by this headhunter to be CEO of some software company, and he asked me out of the blue, 'Have you ever thought of your father's business?' This man knew my father had been in the executive search consulting business.

"I said, 'No, I'd never thought about Dad's business. Guys make lots of money working with my father because he knows people but I don't know anybody.'

"This fellow said, 'Well, it doesn't really work that way.'

"'Really, how's it work?' I asked.

"As he explained the business to me, I went through the mental checklist of what my key criteria were, and lo and behold I realized that the executive search field is, in fact, leadership consulting. That led to where I am now, 20 years later. As my wife says, 'You are in a feel-good business.' If I do what I do well, everyone is happy. The clients are happy because my placement represents exciting new things to come for their business. As a placement, there are few days in your life more exciting than when you land a new job. And guess what? That doesn't happen without me!

"Every few years I reevaluate my life, and it has pretty much remained the same. So far I find that I'm still doing the right thing. If in the future something were to come up that better suits my life assessment criteria, then fine, I'll go do that. But every evening I ask myself if I'm still doing what I want. The answer is unequivocally 'Yes.'

"To sum it up I want to be proud of the things I do. I want to be proud of my behaviors. Although I will have transgressions, I'm quick to acknowledge them and to apologize for them and try to make restitution for them. I want to always do the right thing, even if nobody knows it. Those are the things I try to live by now that I didn't know about when I was growing up. I gained that knowledge 20 years ago in my 12-step recovery program, and that's how I try to conduct my life to this day."

It was hard for Jonathan to face some things about himself that he needed to address, such as his problem with alcohol and what he wanted to do with his life. Once he did, however, he was able to take the next steps toward improving himself and living the life he really wanted. All of us have unique issues, but each of us can identify with some of the truths he learned about himself, and we can apply some of the skills he learned to our own lives.

What you see from where you are

There are four perspectives that affect your performance. The four perspectives are meant to work together to keep you growing. When they don't, you set limitations on your life, governors on your growth.

1. How others view you. The opinions of others tend to affect your behavior.

2. How you attempt to make others see you in a certain way. This is an attempt at image management to control first impressions.

3. The way you actually see yourself. You easily see your flaws, the things you'd like to change. Rarely are you satisfied with what you see.

4. Authentic self. It is made up of your loves, strengths, gifts, talents, abilities, passions, fears, hopes, and character. Any of these may be buried far below the surface of your consciousness.

The key to living a life of integrity is to bring these four images into alignment. And the key to that alignment is in discovering your authentic self. Being authentic means that you have a true picture of yourself and then express yourself congruently and consistently to yourself and to others. We use the word "congruent," meaning that you are the same person no matter where you are. You are, as they say, "comfortable in your own skin."

Embrace your past

Knowing where you are and why you are there involves embracing the past. Embracing the things that happened to you is often much easier than embracing the things that happened because of you. Reflecting on the things that happen because of you can often lead to guilt, and as Erma Bombeck loved to say, "Guilt is the gift that keeps on giving." Guilt can lead to self-sabotaging behavior. "So what should I do with the failures in my life?" you may ask. Embrace them.

> We don't know one successful person who hasn't had a share of fumbles, trauma, disappointments, strategic upheavals, and failures.

The key player in counterproductive behavior is denial. The failures of your past should be gently and lovingly embraced— whether they were self-imposed or other-imposed. We don't know one successful person who hasn't had a share of fumbles, trauma, disappointments, strategic upheavals, and failures.

Do you remember New Coke? It was probably one of the biggest flops in the history of marketing, and Sergio Zyman was the man who engineered the strategy. He resigned in disgrace from Coca-Cola. He kicked around for about seven years as a consultant before he was offered another job. Who hired him? Coca-Cola. The president of Coke defended his decision by saying, "We've become uncompetitive by not being tolerant of mistakes. The moment you let avoiding failure become your motivator, you head down the path of inactivity. You can stumble only if you are moving." Look at mistakes or failures as tuition. If you've already paid the tuition, why not get credit for the course?

When the Center for Creative Leadership asked leaders to identify the things that contributed most to their development, they listed four factors:[2]

Personal hardships	**34%**
Challenging assignments	**27%**
Mentoring relationships	**22%**
Structured training and assignments	**17%**

If winning can continue in spite of negative experiences, then why are so many people and organizations slow to see and solve problems? Why do people not learn from mistakes and failures but instead repeat them? It is because of denial. People who are growing are not immune from problems; winning streaks are not trouble-free periods. Growth is impeded when people deny their problems.

Your past gives you an accurate assessment of your present. As odd as it may sound, it helps create the energy that can move you forward to your dreams and aspirations—knowing who you are, where you are, and what you want.

Biosphere 2, built in the late 1980s in the foothills of Arizona, was designed to be an airtight replica of earth's environment (Biosphere 1). The glass-and-frame structure seals in 7,200,000 cubic feet. It contains five different biomes, including a 900,000-gallon ocean, a rain forest, a desert, and agricultural areas, along with a human habitat. On September 26, 1991, a colony of eight people—four men and four women—entered Biosphere 2 with a mandate to live inside the dome for two years with no contact or support from outside. Several months into the first mission, the oxygen level began to fall at a steady rate, forcing the "bionauts" to have oxygen pumped in from the outside. The crew remained inside for two years, but the project lost credibility. The experience was not without valuable lessons. One interesting observation concerned wind and trees. There was no wind inside the Biosphere 2, so the assumption was that the trees would grow quickly—and they did. But they kept falling over before their reproductive age. It appeared that wind was necessary for creating hardy and strong trees. After observation and experimentation it was determined that the lack of wind caused the wood to grow softer than trees of the same species growing in the wild. While there appeared to be an advantage at first, in the long run the lack of pressure and conflict actually weakened them.

When you reflect on your life, you find that your personal hardships and failures become key learning experiences. When you deny or ignore them, your authentic self doesn't have a chance to grow. Your future is sabotaged.

Why do some people deny their past instead of embracing it? Because it's easier to cling to the distortions; it's safer than facing the fear of losing something they perceive as necessary in their lives. Woody Allen made the point in *Annie Hall*, quoting an old joke. A man enters a psychiatrist's office and says to the doctor,

"Doc, my brother's crazy. He thinks he's a chicken." The psychiatrist replies, "Why don't you just have him committed?" The man replies, "I can't! I need the eggs!"

The medical term "iatrogenic" means "physician-induced" illness. Such an illness happens when symptoms or other important pieces of information are overlooked or carelessness distorts the healing process. It happens in lives when you don't embrace the true causes of a problem. It happens when you treat a symptom instead of a fundamental problem. It happens when healthy behaviors are ignored and minimized. It happens when you close yourself off from valuable feedback, when accountability systems are ignored or eliminated. It happens when you forget that simple but profound truth: The problem named is the problem solved.

When you fail to investigate where you are and why you are there, you are like a physician who is treating only the symptoms, ignoring the fundamental causes, and as a result is making his patient sick. The physician who sees the patient as a whole, looks at his or her history, evaluates the tests, and asks about his or her environment—that doctor is in a much better position to guide the patient to a healthy life. You can become your own best physician by doing likewise, by interrogating your reality to create a healthy life, an authentic life.

The blue pill or the red pill?

In the movie *The Matrix*, Neo (played by Keanu Reeves) suspects there's more to life than what he's experiencing. He suspects that people are complacently accepting the scripts that have been written for them, an illusion.

Morpheus (played by Laurence Fishburne) says to Neo, "I imagine that right now you're feeling a bit like Alice—tumbling down the rabbit hole."

"You could say that," says Neo.

"Let me tell you why you are here," Morpheus says. "You're here because you know something. What you know, you can't explain. But you feel it. You've felt it your entire life—that there's something wrong with the world. You don't know what it is, but it's there. Like a splinter in your mind—driving you mad. It's this feeling that has brought you to me. Do you know what I'm talking about?"

Neo: "The Matrix?"

Morpheus: "Do you want to know what it is?" Neo nods his head. Morpheus says, "The Matrix is everywhere, all around us. Even now, in this very room. You can see it when you look out your window or when you turn on your television. You can feel it when you go to work or when you go to church or when you pay your taxes. It's the world that has been pulled over your eyes to blind you from the truth."

"What truth?" asks Neo.

Morpheus: "That you are a slave, Neo. Like everyone else, you were born into bondage, born into a prison that you cannot smell or taste or touch. A prison of the mind. Unfortunately no one can be told what the matrix is. You have to see it for yourself. This is your last chance. After this there is no turning back."

Then in his left hand Morpheus shows a blue pill. He says, "You can take the blue pill, and the story ends. You wake up in your bed and believe whatever you want to believe." Then he shows him a red pill in his right hand. "You can take the red pill and stay in Wonderland, and I'll show you how deep the rabbit hole goes."

There's a long pause, then Neo reaches for the red pill.

Morpheus says, "Remember—all I am offering is truth, nothing more."

The principle of the Matrix is that you can live a life of illusion, believing that your preconceived limitations are real. You can numb yourself to believe that who you are and what you want are no more, no less, than what you see and experience right now. We are convinced, however, that you intuitively know and feel there's more. Maybe, like Neo, you can't articulate it. But you sense it. You've even felt it at times. The blue pill is denial of the truth and a refusal to embrace your past as a key to your future. It keeps you in a world of illusion. It's time to take the red pill—the truth pill. Where are you and why are you there? Morpheus warned Neo that it wouldn't be easy—at some points even painful. But embracing your current reality is the most liberating feeling in the world. It leads to the joy of living connected to your strengths, passions, and values.

For Reflection

Take an honest look at the difference between what you say and what you do. Think back on your choices and decisions—the thoughts, behaviors, and actions that influenced you and got you where you are today. By aligning your real self, your perceived self, and your ideal self, you can renew your life as more authentic and genuine, so that no matter where you are or what you're doing, you'll be comfortable in your own skin.

The questions that follow will help you accurately describe where you are. They will help eliminate any shadows or fears that have had any hold on what you do and say.

1. Where do I feel stuck?
2. What truth about my life do I avoid exploring? Why?
3. What decisions and choices brought me to where I am today? Do I see a repeated pattern or theme? Would I repeat that today?
4. What is my source of feedback as I explore these questions?

Chapter 5

The Third Dimension
What Will You Do and How Will You Do It?

We are what we repeatedly do.
Excellence then is not an act, but a habit.

Aristotle

*P*lanning.

Be honest with yourself now. How did you react to that word?

Unfortunately many people seem allergic to the planning process and avoid it whenever possible. Why? Some believe that planning requires too much effort and that it takes too much time out of their already busy schedules. Others consider plans to be too inflexible and quickly irrelevant in a fast-changing world. Still others are afraid to enter into a planning process simply because they don't understand how to do it correctly. Whether or not you actually take the time to do it, planning the path to the rest of your life—the best of your life—is essential if you hope to have a chance of achieving what you want in life.

Mastering life requires creating and utilizing a plan for traveling from where you are today to where you want to be tomorrow. This is accomplished by asking the question, "What will I do and how will I do it?"

Answering the question

Trudy Atchison, a high school teacher who today works with at-risk students, asked herself that question 20 years ago. She discovered that once she'd figured out who she was and what she wanted, the answer was simple.

"My first attempt at a college education was in Philadelphia back in the late 1960s. The Vietnam War was going on, and it seemed war protests on campuses occupied the attention of most students. Everything, especially attending class, seemed so meaningless." Eventually Trudy dropped out of college and moved first to New York City, then to California.

"My first job in California was as a waitress at the original Brown Derby restaurant in Los Angeles. One day while working on the outside patio with another waitress who was at least 60 years old, I thought, 'Oh my, what if I'm still doing this when I'm 60 years old?' At the time, I was enjoying the work, earning good money, and felt OK with my job. But it scared me to think of being a waitress all my life. Things were slow before the lunch crowd started to show up, so we began talking. I asked her, 'Did you always want to be a waitress?'

"She looked me in the eye and said, 'No. I didn't want to do this all my life, but this was the only job I could get. I don't have any education. What you need to do,' she said, '—and I give this advice to every young girl who works here—is think about what you really love to do, then do it. You'll always be doing something you really love, and it won't feel like work.'

"That was such simple, great advice. The hard part was that I didn't know what I loved or know what I wanted to do! However her words of wisdom always remained in my thoughts. Finding and deciding on the one thing I loved to do was a concept that I hadn't seriously considered. There had been times in my life when I'd thought, 'Oh, it would be nice to be a teacher,' but I didn't think I was smart enough.

"Several years later I was listening to a call-in radio show, and one of the callers said, 'I can't get a good job because I don't have an education.' The host said, 'You can go back to school; you can go to college. Even if it takes you 10 years, you can finish college if you go part-time at night. Many people have done it.' The caller said, 'Oh, I couldn't do that.' To which the host replied, 'What are you going to do in 10 years if you don't?'

"That really made me think. I told my daughter, who was 9 at the time, 'I'm thinking of going back to college to get a degree in a field that I really like.'

"She looked at me and said, 'Why don't you just become a teacher? You like bossing people around and telling them what to do.'

"I thought, 'If I'm going to make the change, then I'm going to make it now. This is it.' I was in my forties. Fortunately my family supported my decision and helped me with their encouraging words. Once the idea was out, it became obvious not only to me but to everyone around me that I had made the right decision.

"I made immediate changes to cut down my expenses. I used my savings to pay off my credit card debt. I applied for every college grant and scholarship that was available. I took out student loans. I advertised for a roommate to use the spare bedroom. Eventually my daughter and I moved to a smaller place closer to my parents so my daughter would have supervision on the nights I attended classes.

"At first I attended school part time and then full time, graduated with a bachelor's degree, and earned my teaching credential. I received a master's degree while I was teaching full-time.

"I was disappointed when I wasn't immediately hired. I worked as a personal assistant while also working as a substitute teacher for about two years. The pay was terrible, and the benefits were nonexistent. I didn't mind waking up every morning before the crack of dawn to listen to the taped message of substitute teacher openings for the day. I was concerned but kept plugging along. I knew I would find the right position, or it would find me!

"At one point I substituted in the juvenile court schools. I immediately realized that I had found an organization to which I wanted to devote my energies. I was impressed by the dedication and support that was given to students who were having difficulties, including teen pregnancy, gang involvement, anger management, drug and alcohol abuse, sexual abuse, abandonment, and homelessness. These schools treated those kids with respect and with love. Working there was very rewarding, and eventually I was offered a contract. I was thrilled!

"When I look back I realize that all of my experiences, especially the jobs I'd had, helped me become a good teacher. I knew I'd be paying the loans off for quite a while, but I believed it was a good investment. I was making an investment in me, not for something like a car that I would drive only for five or six years but for me—permanently. I was investing in an opportunity to do what I loved.

"Everyone wakes up at a different time and in a different moment. Sometimes a person is there for somebody else, just like the waitress at the Brown Derby was there for me when she helped alter the direction of my life. Now I have the best job in the world. I have the opportunity every day to be there for my students. I love my job and I love my students. And I am happier today than I ever dreamed possible."

Within a few years of landing what she describes as "the best job in the world," Trudy was nominated by the San Diego school system for Teacher of the Year. When you are living the best of your life, it gets noticed!

Create a plan for life

In this chapter you'll learn how to create a plan for your life and how to deal with some of the obstacles you can expect to face. You'll know how to create your own agenda or road map for your life. That road map is a plan, preferably a written plan. Studies show that putting plans into writing and reviewing them frequently increases the probability of achieving them by an average of 35 percent. A written plan is not just something that's nice to do; it's an essential element in your success.

When you read the words "plan" or "planning," what first comes to mind? Depending on your personal experience with the planning process, whether at work or in your personal life, you may cringe at the thought of creating formal, written plans. Why? Probably because you've been involved in some so-called planning process at work or in a community group. You ended up wasting time in countless meetings that never seemed to go anywhere. Or perhaps your efforts produced some grandiose vision that ended up in a three-ring binder gathering dust on a shelf somewhere. That sort of activity in fact is not planning. Someone might have called it "planning," but it wasn't.

Here are some other common reasons people give for avoiding the planning process:

"I don't have time."

"By the time the plan's completed, it's already out-of-date."

"The process is too much work and it takes too long."

"I already have a plan—it's right here in my head."

Planning is an essential tool that contributes to your long-term sense of well-being and fulfillment. Your ability to anticipate, take action, and capitalize on opportunities helps sharpen your skills and dramatically increases your probability of success—because you have a plan.

People who plan make comments like these:

"I'm glad I took the necessary time in the beginning because I saved many times over that in the end."

"I met my schedule because it was flexible and I was adaptable."

"I was surprised at how many problems I could handle along the way because I anticipated most of them ahead of time."

"It's amazing how many great new and unexpected opportunities came my way just because I had a well-thought-out plan and was able to articulate it."

"My goals became a rock-solid reality because everyone around me was able to take them as seriously as I did."

Real and lasting success doesn't happen merely by chance; it's the result of planned decisions and actions. It's the only effective way to create and manage change in our lives, the only way to make the course corrections needed to stay on course for the best of your life.

Understanding why people don't change

Earlier we examined several reasons why people don't change. Two of the major reasons are a fear of change and a perception of a lack of alternatives. We have observed over the years, perhaps surprisingly, that the perception of a lack of alternatives is by far the more debilitating. Fear can be overcome, but that misperception causes people to become stuck and lose hope. When it comes to change, people need as much insight as possible. To help create alternatives for change, we find it very helpful when people understand the forces involved in change. Being able to identify these forces helps to overcome them. A great tool in understanding the forces involved to create change personally or in groups is a system described as Force Field Analysis, developed by social psychologist Kurt Lewin.[1]

> Real and lasting success doesn't happen merely by chance; it's the result of planned decisions and actions.

Any issue, be it a behavior, idea, or desired outcome, is held in balance—what Lewin calls equilibrium—by two opposing forces. The forces promoting change are held in equilibrium or balance by the forces maintaining the status quo. So your status quo behavior is not static; it is being held in place by opposite forces—the driving forces for change and the restraining forces against change. The forces are made up of beliefs, cultural norms, values, expectations, behaviors, habits, moods, needs, anxieties, ideals, goals, and the like. They are pushing against each other to create the point you're at right now.

These forces are always at work in what Lewin referred to as life space—the place where people live their lives. These forces are a part of all humans' lives, whether they recognize it or not. These forces never go away. Weakening or strengthening them is what shifts the equilibrium in one direction or another and produces change.

Force Field Analysis helps demystify change. It helps accurately describe the forces that are in effect when you attempt to make a personal change. With some thought, reflection, and a little analysis, you can begin to clearly see the forces, and once you identify them, controlling them is much easier.

Typical Forces at Work

Driving Forces	Restraining Forces
Felt Need to Change	Belief That Things Won't Change
Negative Consequences	Minimize Consequences
Personal Crisis	Overwhelming Solution Logistics
Advantages of Change	Financial Barriers
New Opportunities	Rigidity
Excitement	Apathy
Relational Cohesion	Conflicting Needs of Others

In the model if the restraining forces that push against change are equal to the driving forces that push for change, change will not occur. The forces for change must be stronger than the forces against change. The best way to do this is first to attempt to remove or weaken the restraining forces. If you weaken or remove the restraining forces, the result will be the desired change. When setting personal goals the best way to create change is to first identify and then eliminate or weaken the restraining forces.

Putting it all to work

To see how this works, take a sheet of paper and title it with a particular behavior you'd like to change. Then create two columns under the heading. In the left-hand column list all the driving forces you can think of in favor of change. In the right-hand column list the restraining forces, everything that prevents this change. For example perhaps you've tried several times to quit smoking. Some of the driving forces in favor of change would be improved health, including lower blood pressure and reduced risk of heart and lung disease; financial savings; lower dry-cleaning bills; smelling better; setting a better example for your children and workmates. Restraining forces would include fear of weight gain, what to do instead with your hands or with your break times, social friction or lack of relationship with coworkers who smoke, and the known nicotine withdrawal symptoms such as nervousness.

As you fill in your model, the following questions and statements will be helpful to think through your desired change:

What is it you want?

Where are you currently?

What will your life look like if you don't make the change?

What are the outcomes motivating you to change? List them in the left column.	
What are the factors making the change seem difficult? List them in the right column.	
Which forces are real, and which ones are merely perceived to be real?	
Which forces are the most difficult to overcome? Rate them on a scale of 1 to 5, with 1 being the weakest and 5 being the strongest.	
Which forces are the most encouraging? Rate them on a scale of 1 to 5, with 1 being the weakest and 5 being the strongest.	
How can you decrease or minimize the forces on the right and increase or maximize the forces on the left?	

Now create a diagram similar to the one on page 113 (see also page 221). Write the change issue in the middle, between the arrows. List inside the arrows the forces for and the forces against change. Rate each on a scale of 1 to 5: 1 being the weakest to 5 being the strongest. How can you weaken or even eliminate the restraining forces? How can you strengthen the forces for change?

It's helpful to create as much asymmetry between the "for" and "against" forces as possible. It clarifies how much the forces are at work in your environment and allows you more insight into how change can and will occur. You will find it more helpful when you can see the balance of power, the participants involved, your adversaries and allies, and your potential to influence all those forces.

This exercise will help you see the alternatives you truly have to bring about change in your life. It will also lessen your assumptions and your fear of change as you see more clearly all the issues involved. It makes it easier to make a change that will take you in the direction of what you want.

It's much easier to begin the planning process once you understand the dynamics of change. Plans and goals always involve some degree of change, so understanding the forces of change involved gives you a tremendous advantage in achieving your goals.

Warning signs that you're not planning

Maybe you think you're already doing a great job planning—and maybe you are. But are you really sure? Or is there room for improvement? You may have all the best intentions when it comes to planning, but if it's not happening, you're not growing. Here are several warning signs by which you can judge the effectiveness of your planning process:

When someone comes with an urgent problem, you act before you think.

You're bogged down in details with no time for looking at the bigger picture.

There are too many options and you become confused about how to reach an outcome.

Instead of anticipating problems before they happen and preparing viable solutions to avoid or handle them, you're busy putting out brush fires.

Others set your agenda and priorities for you.

The same issues and problems keep coming back morphed, regardless of how many times you think you've solved them.

You're surprised when things don't go the way you expect.

When opportunities arise you're too busy to recognize or capitalize on them.

Why set goals?

Without goals you have nothing to plan. Plans are simply the implementations of specific goals you set for yourself. If you want to lose 5 or 50 pounds, you set that goal into motion by placing your new exercise and weight loss routine into your daily schedule. If your goal is to buy a new home, your plan begins by surveying and listing your current sources of income for a down payment, mortgage, insurance, monthly maintenance and utility fees, landscaping, redecorating, renovations, cost of a move, neighborhood schools and attractions, and other factors.

You can choose to be casual about setting your goals, but the more casual you are the less chance your dreams have of ever becoming realities.

If you're still wondering why you should set definite goals in your life, and why goals are important stepping-stones in your journey to self-leadership, then consider the following reasons:

Goals provide direction. To get something done have a clear vision of what your future looks like. By honestly picturing and describing your ideal future, you can translate this destination into goals that will take you exactly where you want to go. Without goals you can end up anywhere; with goals you make choices to do the things that will move you toward your destination.

Goals tell you how far you have traveled. Goals provide milestones along the road to accomplishing your vision. If you determine that you must accomplish seven separate goals to reach your final destination and you complete four of them, you know that you have only three more to go.

Goals help make your vision attainable. By breaking your plans down into smaller steps or tasks that—when accomplished individually—add up to big results, goals help make your overall vision attainable. Your end goals will help motivate you and make it seem easier to go the distance. It's unlikely that you'll be able to attain your vision in one big step; taking a lot of small steps makes accomplishing your goals much easier.

Goals give you something to strive for. It's a fact: People are more motivated when challenged to attain a goal that is beyond their normal level of performance. Not only do goals give people a sense of purpose, but also they relieve the boredom that can come from living a life without challenge.

Step-by-step toward a goal

Football placekicker Rolf Benirschke is one of the most beloved San Diego Chargers of all time. He played 10 seasons in the NFL before retiring at that time as the third-most-accurate kicker in NFL history. He is one of only 33 players to date to be elected to the Chargers' Hall of Fame. For Rolf, however, the challenges of a life-threatening illness are almost as well chronicled as his exploits on the gridiron. Overcoming them took step-by-step determination to reach a goal.

"In my second season I was misdiagnosed with Crohn's disease," Rolf says. "Four surgeries and four years later it was determined my condition was colitis, not Crohn's disease. But during that time I got sicker and sicker, though I continued to play. On Sunday after a game, I'd be taken to the hospital, have an IV placed in my neck, and stay there all week. I'd be released on Saturday to go spend the night with the team. I would wake up Sunday morning, play the game, and then go back into the hospital. For a month I was pretty much fed intravenously. But I maintained my job kicking, and in the 10 years that I played, it was statistically the best of my career.

"In football you are either the starting kicker or you are unemployed, and so my motive was to get to the end of the season. My fear was that I would be called upon to kick a long field goal and not have the strength to do it, but I was making everything. The coach was very understanding. He said, 'Do whatever you need.' I was in the hospital and unable to practice. They allowed me to do that! The next year I remember vividly the opening game. We played in Seattle, and I kicked four field goals. But after every one of them, I had to go to the bench. It was like somebody had stuck a knife in my stomach.

"We'd win the game, and in the locker room everyone was excited and happy. I'd be in front of my locker crying because I knew the end was coming. I didn't know if my illness would be any less if I wasn't playing football, so I just kept going.

"Four games into the season, coming home from New England I collapsed on the plane. I had a 105-degree fever; my colon had perforated and I was taken to a hospital. They did emergency surgery. Six days later they had to do a second surgery, and I woke up with two colostomy bags on my side with my abdomen sewn together with wire. The doctors weren't sure if I was going to live. I was in the hospital for seven weeks. I survived.

"If I were to ask myself—and I did quietly—the rational question, 'Do you ever think you will play football again?' the answer would have been overwhelmingly 'There's no chance that I will ever play again with these bags on my side, with my cut-up stomach, weighing 123 pounds. It's over.' But I didn't think that. I was reduced to simply asking, 'How do I get through the day?' My mother used to say, 'Rolf, don't look at the top of the mountain; just understand it takes little steps to get there. Keep your head down.'

"So what I began to do was every day before anything, I'd get out of bed. That was a challenge, to get out of bed. I had to roll out of bed. I would walk to my neighbor's mailbox and back, and the next day I would walk two mailboxes, and then three mailboxes, and then four. In a couple of weeks, I was walking to the end of the street and back. It really wasn't a walk; it was sort of a shuffle. I couldn't even stand up straight; I just shuffled along.

"I was invited back to watch a game—my first real outing— and I didn't know how I could do it. I could hardly walk. I was upstairs in the press box and was asked if I would visit the team in the locker room. I looked like I'd just come out of a famine or a concentration camp. I was a stick of a human being, but my team-mates were so welcoming. Even so, I could see the horror in their faces because they hadn't seen me for a couple of months.

> "I discovered who I was and what I wanted, at a deeper level than ever before." —Rolf Benirschke

"That's when this big defensive tackle we had from Texas, a guy named Louie Kelcher, 350 pounds, went to coach Don Coryell and said, 'We'd like to make Rolf honorary captain for the day.' That meant I'd have to walk out on the field for the coin toss. I wasn't sure I could. Louie said, 'If you can't walk we'll just have to carry you.' So we got to the sidelines, they called for the captains, and we started walking on the field. The public address announcer introduced the captains. When my name was mentioned everyone in the stadium stood and cheered.

"It was overwhelming. By the time I got to midfield I was in tears. Later the training coach for the team called and said, 'Let's start getting you back in shape.' I was so weak I couldn't bench press the bar. That is when I discovered who I really was and what I wanted, at a deeper level than ever before. In my mind I quit 100 times; my will kept going."

Three steps to victory

"I began to read inspirational books," Rolf says. "*Beyond Survival* by Gerald Coffee, one of the longest-held POWs in Vietnam, talked about the need to break time down into bite-size increments. For POWs it was how they got through the day: all the tortures, all the abuse, bad food, and then knowing that tomorrow would be more of the same. They would just think about 'tomorrow, tomorrow.' Coffee wrote that if someone had told him he would be there seven years and three months, there was no way he would have survived. But he mentally said, 'How do I get through the day?'

"The second thing Coffee wrote was 'We discovered this indomitable spirit that God has gifted each one of us with: the great ability to cope, to persevere, the amount of courage, the great amount of creativity that we all have. It is latent in many of us. It doesn't come out until you are really tested.' I began to relate. I began to discover that same thing.

"Third he said, 'We learned how critical it was to support each other as more and more of us came along in the camp.' For me one day turned into a week, which turned into a month, and all of a sudden it was July and training camp began and I was as strong as I'd ever been. I could kick again, and my colostomy bag stayed on! I went to the owner and said, 'I know there has been a lot of public support for me. You have a team that has a great chance to get deep in the playoffs. I'm asking, Will you allow me to try out for my job? No special favors.' He talked to Coach Coryell, and together they said, 'Yes, as long as you can protect yourself.' It was the Hall of Fame Game, a preseason game, 97 degrees, and it began to rain, but my bag stayed on.

"Then an unusual thing happened. The second-to-the-last preseason game we were playing in LA against the Rams. There were three seconds to go before halftime, and we had the ball. Our drive had stalled, so the coach called the punt team and he turned and walked away. Our special teams coach, who really had gotten to know me, had seen how hard I'd worked out, and saw how strong I was, asked me, 'Rolf, can you make this?' It would be a 55-yard field goal.

"I said, 'I can make this.'

"So he quietly said, 'Field goal team.' The field goal team ran onto the field, and en route we heard Coryell say, 'I said punt team!' We're out there now, and it's too late to come off. I kicked it. It was good. That would be the longest kick in my career. It would demonstrate to them, and to all of us, that I was all the way back. I think I practiced what the Bible prescribes—breaking time down into increments and trusting each day."

Rolf played seven more years, and in a 1982 playoff game against the Miami Dolphins he kicked the winning field goal in one of the most exciting games in NFL history.

Creating a learning agenda

The next step is to possess all the skills needed to fulfill your goals and begin implementing your plans. What if there is a gap between what you know or the skills you have and the information or skills you need? You create a learning agenda for yourself.

Like with any other plan, creating a learning agenda means that you know what your goals are and how you can achieve them. Take the following five steps to create your learning agenda:

1. Determine your goals. While reading Chapter 3 you no doubt began to think about focusing your goals. Now ask yourself: *Where do I want to be next year and the years that follow? What do I need to do to accomplish those goals?* Your answers instantly become your learning agenda.

2. Assess the skills or knowledge you'll need. While some of your goals won't require new skills or knowledge, others will. What specific skills and knowledge do you need to have in order to achieve your goals? What few things keep you from success. What can you do to change for the better? What main skill that you already possess would you like to improve by 25 percent within the next year?

3. Explore the best sources for acquiring the learning. Does that mean going back to school for an advanced degree or attending a community college or adult education program? Enrolling in training offered by your employer? Developing relationships with mentors or coworkers who can teach you the ropes? There is an optimal source for every skill you decide you need to learn. Once you identify the optimal source for any skill you want to learn, it will seem much easier to pursue.

4. Create your learning agenda. Once you've gathered all your information, create a learning agenda—your learning plan—that lays out the skills and knowledge you need to acquire, along with where and when you'll go about it. Put your agenda in writing—there's a much greater chance you'll actually act on your plan if it's in writing than if it's not.

5. Execute. All the learning agendas in the world aren't worth the paper they're printed on if they aren't put into effect. Once you have completed your learning agenda, the fun really begins—you get to put it into action. The sooner you get going, the sooner you'll learn what you have to know and acquire the skills and knowledge you'll need to enjoy and achieve your goals!

SMART goals made easy

You can avoid making plans and you'll still end up somewhere. However that somewhere is unlikely to get you to your goals—in fact you may be led far astray. Decide to set your own agenda and lead yourself through the life that you design. As mentioned before, too many people allow their agenda to be set for them and let others decide where they will—and will not—go. That's not you!

When setting goals doing so in an organized, systematic way works best. In the best-selling book *Putting the One Minute Manager to Work*, Ken Blanchard and Bob Lorber describe the five most important characteristics of well-designed SMART goals:

Specific. Your goals must be clear and unambiguous, in terms that you can easily understand. For example, don't just say "I want to lose weight," write "Reduce my weight by 10 percent." Make goals specific enough to visualize, so you can know exactly what needs to be done when you have completed it.

Measurable. If you can't measure it, you can't manage it. Four key measures provide you real-time feedback : quantity, quality, cost (in money, time, or energy), and time. Measurement helps you understand how far along you are on the path toward reaching your goals, and when your goal is complete—keeping you motivated as you move forward.

Attainable. Successful people set goals that stretch them. But it is a bad idea to set goals that are clearly unrealistic. Why? Because if you know a goal won't be accomplished, you will write it off as unrealistic and won't focus on achieving it. Research shows that goals that are too easy or too hard kill motivation; goals that require some effort beyond your normal comfort zone will motivate you.

Relevant. It's great to have goals, but only if they support your personal vision of the future. If goals have no basis in where you want to be in the future, or if they are designed to satisfy the needs of someone else besides yourself, then you are not being truthful with yourself and you are wasting your time. Every goal you set should be relevant and move you closer to where you really want to be in the future. Remember too the 80/20 rule; focus your efforts on what will provide the most results.

Time-bound. Goals without deadlines are dreams, not reality, and most such goals are fated to never be completed. Inevitably other priorities take over your day, and goals without deadlines get pushed aside so that you can deal with the latest and greatest crisis. Have a timetable and a deadline. Keep a journal or track your progress in a daily planner. Create milestones to manage your journey.

Too many goals can be overwhelming. You are far better off if you set a few significant goals and then concentrate your efforts on attaining them. When it comes to setting goals, less is more.

Promise maker versus promise keeper

When psychologists A. C. Ratzin and D. Payne did research on New Year's resolutions, they discovered that people make the same resolution over and over again.[2] On average, people resolve to stop a particular bad habit 10 times. But a promise maker does not make a promise keeper. After the first week 25 percent of the research subjects gave up. After six months 40 percent had broken their vows. The key to successful promise keeping is to set goals, breaking them into bite-size steps that are doable. As Mark Twain suggested, "The secret to change is one step at a time."

What is it that you need to do this year—the thing that you have delayed and you're in danger of letting roll over into next year? What are you waiting for? Are you procrastinating? Maybe you need to go to somebody and ask for forgiveness. Maybe you need to go to somebody and offer forgiveness. Don't carry resentment, grudges, guilt, or bitterness to the next year. What are those key areas that will contribute to where you want to be?

Turning old habits into new

Practice develops habits, and habits develop attitudes, and attitudes become lifestyles. It's easy to keep doing what you have always been doing. As you become more proficient with new behaviors, you'll find that they take less energy and effort. If you do what you always did, you will always get what you always got. In the words of organizational visionary Max De Pree, "We cannot become what we need to be, remaining what we are."

The best plan is worth nothing if it's not put into practice. Training new habits requires consistent practice—it takes 30 days to turn a conscious behavior into an unconscious behavior (habit). It's like the man who stopped a musician on a New York street and asked him, "How do I get to Carnegie Hall?" The musician replied, "Practice, man—practice."

Catherine Kinney joined the New York Stock Exchange (NYSE) and rose through the ranks, holding management positions in several divisions, including technology planning, sales and marketing, operations, and regulation. During her career with NYSE, her tremendous passion for the company has kept her going. "I have to pinch myself all the time because I am really surprised. I never would have expected myself to have had as long a tenure. It's fun and it's been a great journey. It's been great to be in an organization with a important purpose that's been going on for hundreds of years. It's been a privilege to work with the many people that have been here throughout the years."

Today as president and co-chief operating officer of NYSE Euronext, she knows that she got to where she is now because she made adjustments and improvements along the way. Those were part of her plan in achieving her goals. For example several years ago during a performance review, she received some negative feedback. She could have become defensive or gone into denial, but she immediately accepted the information and created a plan to alter her behavior. Her challenge, interesting enough, was on the subject of change. We have rarely seen someone hit the mark so quickly and so surely. Here's her story:

"We started doing 360-degree assessments when John Thain became CEO. Through that process I received feedback that people didn't think I managed change very well. That startled me because I always thought I contributed a lot to the change process and growth of NYSE, yet it was apparent that people saw me as part of the old school and a little resistant. It was just another reminder that you always have to be of a frame of mind that is capable, prepared, and willing to be flexible.

"Because John was the one delivering the review, I asked him what he thought. We didn't see the written comments, only scores. He was able to explain what was behind the scores. Then I went to two peers whom I really respect and said, 'John shared this score with me. What do you think I should do, or what would you advise me to do?'

"Then I went to two subordinates and said, 'Look, this can be challenging, so I don't want to put you on the spot. For the rest of this year, if you can point out to me moments when you think I am being inflexible, could you leave me a note? It doesn't have to be signed. It will be particularly helpful to me if you give me feedback that's in the moment and really concrete.' I'm better at that than trying to imagine where the situation might be. Instead of being resistant I really try to work on being more flexible and being seen as really trying to be part of a process of change."

Once Catherine had isolated the problem, she dealt with it by putting a system in place that could help train her to catch herself being less open to change. In the process she changed her behavior and positively influenced the opinion of others toward her.

Turning conscious behavior into subconscious

Practice doesn't make perfect—practice makes permanent. Perfect practice makes perfect behavior. If you are honest with yourself, that truth will ensure you are doing the right things. You can't expect to achieve "A" results by doing "B" behavior.

For a behavior to become automatic—and therefore a habit—requires a physical reconfiguring of the brain and then mastery. Mastery comes at the level of implicit learning, which simply means it's coming from within. After you perform a new (conscious) behavior a number of times, it becomes subconscious behavior and becomes automatic and virtually effortless. In six months you won't think completing that behavior is a big deal anymore.

Doing unfamiliar things in unnatural ways causes discomfort to varying degrees. The lack of predictability and control at best is tedious and at worst torture. Less-than-perfect results can be discouraging—especially as you begin the process. As an experiment throw a ball to a friend. Now using your other hand throw the ball again. How did that feel? Did you feel less powerful? Incompetent? Impotent? Would your natural inclination be to fall back on old ways of doing things? Were you discouraged? If your answers to these questions were "yes," then welcome to the world of habit development.

Reviewing goals and schedules

Now is a good time to review any goals you may have created in the past. Are they SMART goals? Is there congruity between your values and your goals? Are they aligned? Do the goals fit into your schedule? Are they achievable? If so, great—move forward. If not, then rework them. Ask yourself if your schedule reflects who you are and what you want. Don't let other people set your agenda. Ask yourself, "Why am I doing this?"

Why? Because as time passes motivation fades and it's easy to forget the original reason behind the goals you selected. So remind yourself, inspire yourself—there is great value and dignity in learning from yourself. You are your own best teacher.

Give yourself a pep talk. Rework your goals into smaller steps if necessary. And remember: Goals you put into writing are goals that you accomplish.

Living your values

Frances Hesselbein is the chairman of the Board of Governors of the Leader to Leader Institute (formerly the Peter F. Drucker Foundation for Nonprofit Management). She was awarded the Presidential Medal of Freedom, the United States of America's highest civilian honor, recognizing her leadership as chief executive officer of Girl Scouts of the USA from 1976 to 1990 and as a pioneer for women, diversity, and inclusion.

For Frances Hesselbein living by core values is something to always strive for. Frances says, "You always remain faithful to the values you try to live by. I had a very touching experience three years ago when I was speaking on challenges of leadership in the 21st century in three different cities in China. We reached 2,000 business, government, and nonprofit leaders in that week in Beijing, Shenzhen, and Dongguan. Before I went I met with Chairman Shao Ming Lo, a business leader in China who is dedicated to supporting education in many ways. I said, 'There's one word I would like to ask you about because I don't want to use a word that would be awkward or embarrassing. At the end of my speech, I would like to say, "We keep the faith," speaking of leaders. How does that translate?' And Chairman Shao Ming Lo said, 'Oh, please use that, for in Chinese "faith" translates as "truth." ' I think today there is a hunger for truth.

"We must first and foremost be truthful with ourselves. That truth must translate into behaviors, and this is where good habits are essential."

Rehearsing new behaviors until they are automatic

The more you rehearse your new behaviors by putting them into practice as often as possible, the quicker and easier it will be to adopt them permanently. Ready to start?

Step 1: Pick a particular new behavior that you want to turn into a habit. Express it in writing in the form of a positive goal. Let's say, for example, that you want to spend more time with your family and less time at the office. A positive way to practice this new behavior would be to write, "I will leave the office every day by 6:00 p.m."

Step 2: Repeat your written goal to yourself as often as you possibly can while visualizing yourself doing the exact behavior that you have written out and are affirming to yourself. Be positive, be excited. You are programming your subconscious mind to think in terms of the new behavior, and once you have your subconscious mind thinking in those terms, your conscious mind will soon follow.

Step 3: Commit yourself to your new behavior by performing it whenever it is appropriate to do so. Make a conscious effort to catch yourself doing the old behavior and then replace the old behavior with the new one. Remember: The more often you actually do the new behavior, the faster (and more easily) it will become a habit.

Step 4: Let others know that you are committed to a new behavior and encourage them to tell you when you have fallen back into your old behavior. Not only do you provide yourself with additional motivation to create a new habit by telling others about your goal (you want them to see you succeed), but you set up a feedback loop that will tell you truthfully when you have stepped out of line.

Step 5: Keep track of your progress. Every day assess whether or not you are performing your new behavior. If so, great! Celebrate and keep on doing what you're doing. If not, figure out why not and take steps to get back on track. Simply recommit to your goal and keep plugging away. Perseverance will eventually win the day.

For Reflection

Plans and goals are the most reliable way to move from your current reality to where you want to be in the future—to get you from here to there. Begin the planning process by asking yourself the following questions:

1. Set three goals in your life: one each for your work life, your family life, and your personal life. Make sure they are Specific, Measurable, Attainable, Relevant, and Time-bound.

2. What skills would I like to increase by 25 percent during the next year?

3. What are three habits that will assist me in getting where I want to be?

4. What will I do differently starting today?

5. What are the restraining forces that hinder my progress?

6. What are the driving forces that will help me follow through on my goals?

Chapter 6

The Fourth Dimension
Who Are Your Allies and How Can They Help?

Two are better than one, because they have
a good return for their work: If one falls down,
his friend can help him up. But pity the man
who falls and has no one to help him up!

Solomon (Ecclesiastes 4:9–10)

"Gentlemen, I don't want to hear what we can't do. I want you to tell me what we can do—and failure is not an option." Gene Kranz, flight director of NASA's Mission Control, spoke in firm, measured voice to the room full of engineers after an explosion crippled the *Apollo 13* spacecraft. His sobering words galvanized four teams into action to save the lives of three astronauts hurtling through space 200,000 miles away.

It's hard to imagine a more complicated set of problems in a more critical situation. On board the Apollo craft, an electrical short had caused an explosion in the oxygen tanks. John Swigert, feeling the explosion and seeing a warning light blink on, delivered one of the most eloquent SOS calls of all time: "Houston, we've had a problem." More warning lights turned on, signaling the loss of two of the three fuel cells as gas—oxygen—began escaping from the second and last tanks. The failures multiplied: a loss of electricity, light, water, and power, and those were merely the most comprehendible of the myriad technical issues. Any prospect of a lunar landing was rendered impossible.

Back in Houston Kranz's White Team at Mission Control was about to be relieved from monitoring the mission by the Black Team, directed by Glynn Lunney, when the "problem" occurred. Kranz, "boss of bosses," immediately reorganized the schedule so that Lunney's Black Team, Gerry Griffin's Gold Team, and Milt Windler's Maroon Team began to monitor the mission, while his White Team became the offline Tiger Team to focus, analyze, and offer solutions. Kranz then focused on keeping the exhausted, dehydrated crew awake as much as possible in the cold, darkened craft as he shifted the mission from a lunar landing to survival and return.

The four teams collected duplicates of every tool, material, and piece of equipment to be found on the capsule in a room—nothing more, nothing less—and working with the astronauts they came up with a plan that saved the lives of the *Apollo 13* astronauts James Lovell, John Swigert, and Fred Haise. This incredible display of imagination could never have come from a single individual. It was the synergy among dozens on the ground and three astronauts in space, making the whole greater than the sum of its parts. Against all odds *Apollo 13* returned and landed safely in the Pacific Ocean 88 hours later.

The following day President Richard Nixon awarded Kranz and the three other flight directors the Presidential Medal of Freedom. Two weeks later they followed the astronauts in a ticker-tape parade in Chicago.

Kranz's powerful yet vulnerable words rallied a diverse group of experts to strive in the face of the overwhelming odds. Commander Lovell later credited Kranz's ability to surround himself with good people with the lifesaving success. "Kranz didn't have the answers. But he was able to leverage the strengths, insight, and wisdom of those around him to avert disaster."

Too often instead of enlisting help, people are more concerned with how they believe others will perceive them if they ask for help. Does asking for help indicate you're in trouble, that you're going under, or you're weak and in a particularly vulnerable, dire state? Does it mean you can't take care of yourself or didn't prepare enough? If you were drowning in the ocean, would you call out to a lifeguard for help or berate yourself for all the swimming classes you didn't take? Or wonder what the lifeguard might think about the dire situation you're in? No question you'd signal for help and not care one iota about much of anything else. When you're drowning in a problem, by all means ask for help! And as with the lifeguard, you trust that person and give him or her the chance to use the skills he or she has honed to be useful and helpful to you and others.

When is the last time you heard someone say that he or she learned and experienced all he or she could in order to hoard the information and keep it for himself or herself? Everyone loves being asked for advice because it's an honest compliment, a way of saying, "I trust you and you know more than I do!" Who wouldn't like that?

Success never happens without assistance

While your journey might appear on the surface to be a solitary one, it's not the case. Life is filled with *Apollo 13* "We've had a problem" scenarios, some major, some minor. It's up to us to be ready for everything and anything that comes our way. Once when Bob was on a speaking tour, his colleague Herb Cohen, author of *You Can Negotiate Anything*, emphasized this point: "The four most powerful words in anyone's vocabulary are 'Can you help me?'"

> Surrounding yourself
> with good people and
> harnessing mutual supporters
> is not a sign of weakness;
> it's a sign of strength.

Surrounding yourself with good people and harnessing mutual supporters is not a sign of weakness; it's a sign of strength. Achieving the life you want requires the physical, emotional, psychological, and spiritual support of your family, friends, work associates, mentors, and everyday acquaintances. Mutual support allows you to achieve far more than you ever could on your own. The key to harnessing supporters is trust. And trust is a two-way street. In order to truly trust others, you must be trustworthy. When others trust you they are usually willing to be there for you too. That's why you need to develop mutual supporters. Think of it this way:

Keep Simple Agreements + Do No Harm = Trust

The first part—keep simple agreements—means doing what you say you're going to do. That means keeping all your commitments. If you make a promise with someone and honor that agreement, you strengthen the bond of trust with that person. Break or recklessly postpone a promise and you break a bond. Trust can build for years and evaporate in the blink of an eye. Trust is like a pure mountain stream with a fragile ecological balance. When trust is polluted it takes time and effort to restore. If the trust stream is maintained, the purity is guaranteed.

The second part of the formula—do no harm—means that you won't take advantage of someone's vulnerability when that person places trust in you. It also means that when you trust someone else, you have no pretenses or false fronts, and he or she sees the real, authentic you. When you trust that someone will tell you the unvarnished truth, and that that person will not harm you with the truth about you he or she holds, you both become better for the experience.

Plant seeds of trust

What kind of behavior promotes trust in relationships? Look for these five things: vulnerability, information sharing, empathy, celebration, and encouragement.

Vulnerability. Your friends and associates are drawn to your humility when you let them know you need them. Influential people can always trace both their successes and failures to the relationships in their lives. Successful people's dreams are always bigger than they are. That being the case their choice is either to give up or get help. Successful people realize that others want to be part of a shared vision. You can do the same. Invite others to be a part of your dream, and then let them see how significant their role really is. You give up nothing by doing this. In fact you gain—you gain their trust. People are drawn to others who are open and honest about their need for input.

Information sharing. Whenever you share information especially of a personal nature about yourself to a trusted friend, that act draws the friend in and creates an ally. One important thing is to know when to stop and how to be appropriate to the situation at hand. The information you are sharing should not be more than the depth of the relationship you already have with the person or people. You and your ally have your own set of boundaries. If that person says, "That's more than I needed to know," don't be embarrassed. The statement gives you valid information: You know when the person has heard enough. Say, "Thank you, I appreciate your letting me know your boundaries. I will respect that in the future." An old Sicilian expression says, "Only the spoon knows what is stirring in the pot." When you give another person a taste of what's stirring in you, that person becomes an important part of your life.

Empathy. The ability to understand and be sensitive to others' experiences and feelings is the mark of a mature person. The foremost sign of personal growth is being a good listener and being curious about the innermost passions of friends and associates. Discover their dreams, values, and talents. As you learn their unique perspectives, the common ground between you grows; your points of connection increase. Even one of the toughest, hardest-charging—and most successful—NFL coaches cultivated empathy. Vince Lombardi, the legendary Green Bay Packers coach, once said, "Coaches with the ability to outline plays on the blackboard are a dime a dozen. The ones who succeed are those who can get inside their players and motivate them." Through empathy you motivate others, and you benefit from their success.

Celebration. In a relationship of mutual support, the contributions and successes of others require your recognition. During the first 10 minutes of a conversation, look for opportunities to highlight the other person's progress and achievements. Focus on giving your attention, appreciation, and affirmation. Rather than giving up time to make your points, you are actually gaining. A scarcity mentality says that you lose that portion you give to others. An abundance mentality says that whatever you give to others will come back to you in greater degree. In a trusting environment you will see friends celebrate each other's achievements as their own. You will discover this to be a great source of empowerment and a key to achieving your own clarity of purpose.

> "I will never get from others what I myself am unwilling to give." —Mike Scioscia

Encouragement. When you give encouragement, you get it. It's the real gift that keeps on giving. Encouraging others is a great source of self-encouragement and an investment that compounds interest. Even long after you have forgotten words or notes of encouragement, they are remembered by the recipient.

These five qualities are not just essential ingredients of trust. They are two sides of the same coin. They not only produce trust, but trust in turn promotes these behaviors. Mike Scioscia, manager of the Los Angeles Angels of Anaheim, knows this well. A major-league catcher for 15 years, he was twice a World Series champion with the Dodgers. He was selected Manager of the Year in 2002 when he led the Angels to their first World Series Championship. No one would have predicted this success from the way the team started its season. The Angels began the year by stumbling to a 6-14 start—not exactly a championship march.

Scioscia preaches the importance of surrounding yourself with good people who will not only give you valuable information but also tell you the truth. "We all have blind spots," he says. "The successful person gathers all the information he can, even if it's uncomfortable, even if it's not what you want to hear."

Scioscia is an excellent communicator and in no way sees vulnerability and transparency as signs of weakness. For him they are a major source of strength and essential for his role as a leader. As a result his team trusts him and his philosophy. The players and coaches know that he wants the best for them. He coaches the most out of their talent. Developing trusting relationships is essential to helping players discover who they really are and what they really want. "You have to find and touch the passion they have to play. If you can connect with their love to compete, that passion, a lot of the rest is almost self-generating. They find their roles, and you put them in positions where they can reach their talent level. People have to feel your support and believe that they are something special, or they'll never reach their potential. That's what I want from those supporting me. But I will never get from others what I myself am unwilling to give."

The people working with Mike know that he wants the best for them. He never rips his players in the press or criticizes them in public. Behind closed doors he is firm and direct. As he demonstrates, trust is not soft. It's a simple transaction—you know the formula now: Keeping simple agreements plus doing no harm yields trust.

Trust is the key to mutual support and allows you to achieve far more than you ever could on your own. Antwone Fisher had a difficult time trusting anyone. His mother gave birth to him while she was in prison. His father was shot and killed before Antwone was born. His foster parents mentally and physically abused him over a 14-year period. He eventually graduated from high school and joined the Navy, where he received psychological counseling because of a deep-rooted anger-management issue. The very ideas of trust, mutual supporters, allies, or asking for help—let alone pursuing one's dream—were foreign to Antwone. If he ever trusted anyone in his life, he was quickly punished for it.

While Antwone was in the Navy, his psychologist noticed he had a real talent for writing. He challenged him to develop those strengths and to get in touch with the passions deep within his soul. Antwone's counselor began to instill a sense of trust in him. It was a huge step for Antwone, but he began asking himself who his allies were and how they might help. Mutual supporters were beginning to emerge. Someone even paid his salary for nine months so he could write his autobiography, which became the best-selling book *Finding Fish: A Memoir*, and the film that bears his name. Since then Antwone has become a successful author and screenwriter.

Antwone came to California State University, Long Beach, as the keynote speaker to a standing-room-only crowd of 1,500 students. Speaking to them he emphasized the importance of having mutual supporters. "Look around," he said, "because you're here in part because of mutual supporters." Being aware of the allies who have helped you get where you are today will accelerate your ability in using allies to get where you want to go. Antwone served up a challenge to the students. "Some of you were born on third base. Others on first base. It doesn't matter. You can't help where you start. The question is, What have you done with what you've been given?"

Studies show that most people focus on what they don't have rather than on what they do have. Accept where you are and build from there. Antwone wasn't on third base or first base. In fact he wasn't even in the ballpark. Yet he made it to home plate in part, by his own admission, "because of mutual supporters." Develop the powerful tool of surrounding yourself with allies that provide mutual support.

Winning with people

David Shakarian is a man many would consider to be a business legend. He is the founder of the General Nutrition Corporation (GNC). Today GNC has more than 6,000 stores in the United States and 49 other countries. While Mick was in his mid-twenties, he had the privilege of observing David's business acumen and was enormously impacted by his perspective on relationships.

David told Mick, "Skills and habits are extremely important in building a successful life and sustaining a life mission, but in addition you must consider the people with whom you are surrounded." His success as a businessman was quite impressive. But it wasn't only his business savvy that continued to influence Mick's life. It was David's ability to focus on the key relationships that were needed to support his quest for who he was and what he wanted, both professionally and personally. His principle was simple: "The quality of your life will be in direct proportion to the types of relationships you choose to build." Relationships can help or hinder you. They will help you endure distractions on your journey, or they can be distractions.

One of the great slogans a few decades back was "You are what you eat!," which was also a favorite saying of David's. It's a physical truth; you can quantify it. But David took it one step further when he said, "You are who you eat with. Eating the right kinds of foods is important, but so is engaging the right kinds of friends. This must be intentional."

Studies show that during our teenage years we spend one-third of our time with friends. As we grow to adulthood, work, family, and personal interests increase, and the average time we spend with our friends drops to less than 10 percent. If this is true for you, think about the friends with whom you want to spend that time. Are you seeing them? Or is your calendar filled with appointments with other people, people who want to see you? Pick your friends well and give them your prime times. How do your friends affect your personal and work life? How do they affect your other relationships? If you put all your friends in a room, would they all enjoy the time together? Why? Would you? Why? What do your friends provide you, and what do you offer them in return?

Have a mentor, be a mentor

You have probably heard many times about the value of a mentor, a trusted counselor and guide. We all need one, and at some point we all need to be one. One of the reasons we need mentors is because of the perspective they provide. That perspective comes from different directions. Following are the four basic roles that mentors play:[1]

Upward mentors. These are the people you look up to. They have helped and are still helping you become who you are. They could be a parent, grandparent, coach, author, pastor, or boss. They might be direct mentors or indirect mentors.

Friendship mentors. These are the people that you experience life with. You have gone through various stages with them—college, career, family, and associates. You've learned from them in a give-and-take way. They are not upward mentors. They are side mentors.

Sandpaper mentors. These are also side mentors, but they serve a little different function. You don't have to look for them; they always find you! These are people that rub you the wrong way. They might even be your critics. But in reality they help sharpen you if you are observant, open, and nondefensive. Be open to hear the one or two points in their criticism that are true and learn from those points. Don't reject all that they say simply because they are critics or cranks.

Downward mentors. These are the people you have invested in. They may be younger than you, but not necessarily. When you invest in others in a giving relationship, you actually learn a lot about yourself. When you listen to yourself offer information and insights, it affirms what you believe and know to be true. You see what's important to you and what should be emphasized and reinforced in your own life.

Providing you with patterns

Don't expect your friends, mentors, or advisers to be good at everything simply because they are good at one thing. Studies show that 83 percent of people bring strengths different from their counterparts to a relationship. We often seek in others the qualities we don't have but want for ourselves. No doubt some around you are already where you want to be—financially, emotionally, spiritually, and vocationally. How did they do it? They might not be where you want to be in all areas of life, but you can still learn from their successes in those particular areas. General George Patton wasn't Greek, but he learned from Alexander the Great. Martin Luther King wasn't Hindu, but he learned nonviolent resistance from Gandhi. And Gandhi's role model was Jesus.

People who are different from us can provide us with patterns to help us break out of our comfort zones. They challenge us to take risks—to dream dreams. They help us to break through those barriers once thought impassable. For example, by running the mile in under four minutes, Roger Bannister did what people thought was scientifically impossible. Yet within one year more than a dozen others had done the same thing. Why? Because Bannister showed what was possible, and a new pattern was set. People aren't perfect, but if you are ready and observant, people will provide you with patterns that will help make your journey much easier.

Providing you with instruction

Friends and mentors are the people who bring out the best in you. They are not afraid to tell you the truth. They keep you growing and on track. When you share your goals with them, they, too, are committed to those goals and become actively involved in your efforts. They act like a coach, giving you instruction to stick with your game plan, to perform at your peak. No matter what success you experience, your need for coaching will never diminish.

LeBron James is an extremely successful NBA basketball player. Does he have a coach? Perhaps several? Celine Dion, Barbra Streisand, and Beyoncé Knowles can sing circles around hundreds of other female singers. Yet each woman spends great time and effort to make sure she has the right voice coach. In fact all professionals in all sorts of fields have coaches. That's why they're pros! Successful people at all levels make a habit of sharpening their skills by surrounding themselves with those who can provide instruction and challenge their wits.

Providing you with inspiration

Surround yourself with people who want to help you grow—people who are excited about where you are going. You will gain that reaction from others when you are just as curious and helpful about their welfare as they are about yours.

> Successful people at all levels make a habit of sharpening their skills by surrounding themselves with those who can provide instruction and challenge their wits.

Benjamin Franklin surrounded himself with people he called "my most ingenious friends group." He produced his greatest inventions after he was 70 years old; he was still accomplishing much well into his eighties. He invented the iron furnace stove, called the Franklin Stove, bifocal glasses, the library system that is still in place today, swim fins; and he organized the first fire department, which had as its slogan "An ounce of prevention is worth a pound of cure." Franklin started a fire insurance system that protected businesses and homeowners and became world-famous for demonstrating the connection between electricity and lightning. He credited much of his productivity to the inspiration of his friends, who kept him growing and thinking.

Thomas Edison surrounded himself with people he referred to as "my mastermind alliance." It wasn't Edison who had the main idea behind the lightbulb. It was his alliance. They averaged one minor invention every six weeks and one major invention every six months. They came up with more than 300 inventions in just six years. Friends inspire us. Emerson said, "A true friend is one who makes us do what we can do." They bring out the best in you. They stretch you, press you, nudge you, and don't allow you to stagnate.

Major League Baseball's Pat Gillick, who is now the general manager of the Philadelphia Phillies and was GM of the Seattle Mariners, told us, "You can only accomplish so much. To go beyond your own limitations, you need help. You get that help from those surrounding you: your friends, associates, team, and significant others. So in a way they are as responsible for your success as you are."

> The quality of your life will be in direct proportion to the types of relationships you choose to build.

One supporting friendship is worth a thousand acquaintances. The other side of the coin is also true. Nothing will sabotage your journey for the best of your life as quickly as the wrong friends. The point is that you will never rise above the level of your closest friends. The quality of your life will be in direct proportion to the types of relationships you choose to build.

People were not designed to go it alone. The need for companionship is one of the most fundamental human needs. Even though this is true, many people fail to cultivate supporters or mentors. This unmet need has a negative impact on both their personal and professional lives. Organizations that don't promote this kind of thinking do so at their own peril. According to Tom Rath, author of *Vital Friends: The People You Can't Afford to Live Without*, people who have vital friends at work are seven times more likely to be engaged in their job. They accomplish more in less time, with more innovation, with fewer accidents, producing more engaged customers. Business researchers have discovered that this kind of relationship jumps employee satisfaction by 50 percent.[2]

On another front if your best friend has a healthy diet, you are five times more likely to have a healthy diet yourself. If your best friend is physically active, there's a good chance you are too. Recent studies on obesity show that friends influence each other's weight.

Many tests measure what is called synergistic decisionmaking. They measure the difference between individual decisionmaking and group decisionmaking. In the vast majority of cases, the ability to make good decisions—decisions that are based on accurate information and are also right for you—strengthens when you make decisions as a member of a group that has the same goals and objectives in mind. In the case of these decisionmaking tests, the objective is both survival and success. Your ability to make productive decisions is enhanced when you involve mutual supporters. They are, in fact, your allies and, in some cases, your mentors.

This is all tied in with the basic way people function. One way to look at people's need for relationships is to recognize that there are two great forces in constant dynamic tension in all of us: the force for togetherness and the force for separateness. The two forces need to be kept in balance.

If the force for togetherness becomes too strong, you can become dependent on others for prolonged periods of time, perhaps even a lifetime. Being overly dependent on others can be debilitating, both for you and for the people on whom you depend. When you allow others to do for you what you can do for yourself, you drain your own vision and energy for life. Your overreliance on someone or some group becomes an energy vampire, sucking the vitality out of your life and the lives of your associates. People who are overly dependent are constantly deferring; they sometimes seem immobile until someone tells them what to do. Others view them as needy. They do not see themselves as having control over their own lives. They often blame others for what's happening to them, further abdicating responsibility for their lives. They adopt a victim mentality. Recognize that you will never satisfy their bottomless pit of neediness. When you know that up front, you can choose how to proceed with them.

Codependency is when you fail to draw the distinction between your separateness and your togetherness. Separateness is buried and togetherness is artificially constructed—the relationship's foundation is based on fear. That fear can immobilize you to the point that staying in a negative, undesirable relationship seems more preferable to the unknown future if you tried to break it off—fears like this are subconsciously motivated. The result of codependency is an enmeshed relationship without boundaries. The individual's life is defined by his or her relationship to another person, becoming a spineless codependent who can't say "no." Since they can't control the boundaries of their own life, codependents feel the desire to control the people around them, at home and at work, often taking on responsibility for others as a means of finding their own identity.

A classic example is the spouse of an alcoholic who finds his or her identity in caring for the other person. When the alcoholic recovers, the relationship is at risk because the spouse has lost his or her identity as a caretaker. When children move into adulthood, this is a struggle for many parents whose identity is enmeshed with the identities of their children. When the parent senses a loss of control, he or she also experiences a loss of identity. Parents can go into a depression or have an emotional crisis. Some 50-year-old children have yet to escape the control of their parents. It is possible for both parent and child to struggle with a loss of identity; the result is a codependent relationship.

> Functioning as a fully integrated human being is a matter of knowing where you end and where the other person, group, or organization begins.

Many people go to the opposite extreme: independence. They want to show others and themselves that they are strong. The problem is that they can be alone too long; the force for separateness is out of balance with the force for togetherness. They lose a healthy connection with those around them. In American culture independence is highly valued, which makes it difficult to see the negative aspects of being independent. The danger of independence, however, is isolation from others and, as a result, failure to benefit from the nurturing, love, fun, and insights that come with good relationships.

A healthy balance between separateness and togetherness brings you to the desired level of interdependence. Interdependence is the ability to self-differentiate—knowing where you end and others begin, as well as the ability to recognize the need for others in your life. In a healthy relationship the two parties ought to be able to say to one another, "Since we love, care about, and are committed to one another, I'll take care of me for you, and you take care of you for me." Each loves and cares for the other, but some things one simply can't do for the other person; some responsibilities cannot be shared. And if one person makes the other be responsible for those areas, he or she will feel stuck or perhaps even want out of the relationship. It's unhealthy for both parties and impedes their personal growth.

When you ask the question "Who are my allies and how can they help?" you are not giving up your responsibility for the decisions and choices that you make. You are realizing and acting on the importance that others play in living out the life you want. It's a beautiful, healthy balance, and it is the way relationships at every level were designed to work.

As human beings we were designed to be interdependent with those around us. NASA's Gene Kranz wasn't suddenly interdependent when there was a potential disaster; he built a great team over time to be ready for anything. That's the way he functioned as launch director during the uneventful moments. In fact if interdependence hadn't already become his normal mode of operation, it would never have worked in the crisis

Consider the example of a teenager finally getting her driver's license: More than anything else getting that little laminated sandwich of paper and plastic is an emphatic symbol of independence. But while a driver's license is also the gateway to a new life of independent living, that teenager is actually doing one of the most interdependent functions in which she could be involved. You don't just get in the car and drive. You are dependent first of all on someone making that car, selling the car, pumping oil, refining gas, making sure the stoplights work, and (ideally) repairing the potholes. And don't forget you are also dependent on all the other drivers on the road with you. When someone crosses the line, doesn't pay attention to the accepted rules of the road, runs a stoplight, and crashes into your vehicle, it becomes apparent just how interdependent we are. And of course, that new teenage driver has an effect on you too—if it's your own son or daughter, that new laminate keeps you awake at night, and if it's a neighbor's kid, you're driving defensively!

Just as in driving so also in life: Successful living is accomplished when we are interdependent on our mutual supporters and mentors. They help us with where we are going, why we are going there, and how we are going to get there. They realize our full potential, point out when we are extending our capabilities, and ensure there is value and fulfillment in the work we are accomplishing. Who is going with us is very important in getting to where we want to go. No dream survives a collision with reality, and our mutual supporters—our allies—allow us to see that reality more vividly if we let them.

The final 10 percent

People cannot grow without feedback. So why do so many avoid it? Simple—because feedback can be painful. Hearing the truth about ourselves is simultaneously difficult and rewarding. Most people will tell you 90 percent of what you need to know. That's the easy portion. It's that last 10 percent that makes the biggest difference. You don't necessarily want to hear the bad news, nor do others want to take on the burden of sharing that news. That's where the cultivation of trusted friends pays great dividends. They must be invited in by you. They won't volunteer for this hazardous duty without incentives from you. As Solomon said in Proverbs, "The wounds of a friend are more faithful than the kisses of an enemy." That even applies in baseball!

"Sometimes the very thing that seems to derail us is the catalyst that keeps us on track."

—Pat Gillick

Pat Gillick is now general manager of the Philadelphia Phillies. He has been named Major League Executive of the Year on more than one occasion. Pat says, "Baseball is very much a people business. To be effective baseball players need to know where they stand in their organizations, and they have to be able to completely trust their managers and teammates. This means being as honest and as open as possible.

"About 40 years ago someone told me the truth, and it forever changed my life. I was playing minor league baseball at the time, and I asked the general manager what my chances were of going into the big leagues. He was quite honest with me, even though it wasn't comfortable. He said, 'I would say that you have a slight chance, but in reality not a very good chance of making it to the majors.'"

Pat recalls, "This was not pleasant to hear. It stung. And even though it immobilized me for a time, I knew it was true! Looking back, denying the truth about myself would have handicapped my future success. At that point I made a decision to go to some other aspect of the game. After assessing my skill set along with my passion for baseball, I decided to get into the administrative side of the game. Sometimes the very thing that seems to derail us is the catalyst that keeps us on track.

"Facing the truth was difficult at times, and there were those moments when I wanted to get back on the field. The truth is I probably could have played a couple more years—and possibly missed the opportunity to get into the administrative end of the game. The timing was important. My manager's honest feedback and my willingness to listen eventually opened up a whole new direction for my life." Knowing who you are and having what you want won't happen without seeing your need for allies and understanding that their help includes honest feedback. "One of the keys to my success is to surround myself with people who can give me honest feedback," Pat says. "Detractors are not invited into that circle. I look for mutual supporters. I also look for those people I can learn from, who are in a position to mentor me."

People don't know what they don't know

If people are not honest with who and where they are, they will never arrive at where they want to go. Interrogating reality is not easy—in fact sometimes it is impossible—without the help of mutual supporters, our allies. Feedback about performance and potential is one of the most critical components of personal and professional growth. Nothing happens until growth-minded people gather direct, timely feedback on the things that really matter. But it's not enough to surround yourself with good people—you must be one yourself.

Discovering who you are in relation to others is a key step. One helpful tool for that purpose is the Johari Window, a graphic model of interpersonal awareness, developed by psychologists Joseph Luft and Harry Ingham.[3] It is a model of interpersonal processes that illustrates relationships in terms of awareness and identifies four distinct areas based on oneself and others. Our chart below, based on the Johari Window, describes these interpersonal relationships in similar fashion.

Open and Authentic	My Blind Spots
"What you see is what you get." I know myself and allow others to know me exactly the way I am.	What others see in me but I don't or can't see about myself
My Secret Self	My Hidden Potential
What I know about myself and what others don't know about me	What others don't see in me and I don't yet know about myself

Discovering who I am

All people's lives have an open area. The transparent part of their lives is the open window that lets the fresh air in and is completely open to the outside world. They are completely comfortable with the exposure, and it can be as mundane as the talking-about-the-weather part of our lives. It's open and free.

Everyone has a blind area in his or her life. When we talk about blind spots, we are talking about behaviors that others see but of which individuals themselves are unaware. It's like having bad breath or spinach in your teeth: Everybody knows it but you. For example others may see you as intense while you fail to see that particular behavior in yourself; you think you're easygoing. The key is to hear this information from others, listen to it, and then do something about it.

The secret area is where you avoid revealing to others—things you know about yourself—your little secrets or skeletons in your closet. It could be something serious that if known could get you fired, divorced, or bankrupt. It might be a hidden agenda you have that can gain an advantage over someone else. Or it may be withholding information about yourself that you are sensitive or embarrassed about.

The area of hidden potential is where neither you nor other individuals are aware of your motives or behaviors. This is also the area of potentially your greatest growth. This is where much of your untapped potential lies dormant. This is the area of your life where you can "re-spirit" and refocus where you are going. This area tends to remain hidden—just below the area of consciousness—but it is very influential.

Self-talk is the internal dialogue going on in every person's hidden area. Although other people's input is influential, the input you give yourself has even more impact. During stressful, anxious times the input can be negative or deceptive. Alternately, it is easy to engage in pipedreams, rooting your internal dialogue in illusion. What we've found is that most people's internal dialogue does not reflect reality. Reality-based self-talk, however, deals honestly and objectively with what's going on.

Monitor your self-talk. Keep track of what you are saying to yourself. As you reflect on your past and remake your future, listen to the way you talk to yourself. Is it positive or negative? For example, let's say you were in a department meeting and made an ill-timed or unproductive comment. When you hear in your head something like "I made a really bad mistake," don't beat yourself up over the situation. Instead say to yourself: "Now I know what not to do next time." Or perhaps your inner voice tells you, "That was a really dumb thing I said in the meeting." Instead think, "Wait, it's not like it was the last meeting I'll go to this week. I'll think of something brilliant to say next time—and from now on I'll think before I blurt something out. Today I learned a valuable lesson." Maybe you tell yourself, "I am so mad at myself for being late." Counter that with positive self talk, such as "I have to change this pattern because it's not doing me any good. Easy solution: from now on I'll be early!" In your hidden areas lies an incredible amount of adventure and enjoyment just waiting to be discovered! Your best potential is always there, but it is sometimes hidden and waiting to be found. You don't want to be like the person who barely scratches out a living trying to grow crops on arid, rocky soil, when in fact there's oil underneath the land. You won't be living in poverty because you will mine the millions of dollars' worth of wealth that's already there. Your mutual supporters are the geologists who will guide you in tapping your personal wealth.

The key to understanding all these parts of the Johari window is the open area. As the open area expands, you have fewer blind spots, less hidden area, and less unknown area. There is more congruity and alignment in your life. That's when you become whole. That's when the idea of who you want to be more closely matches who you are.

You can't deal with the blind area, the hidden area, or the unknown area without other people in your life. Dealing with those areas requires feedback that is both truthful and candid from mutual supporters. And those relationships are based on trust. Exposure is not easy; without trust it won't happen. When you tell others your dreams, your true desires, your goals, and your vision for the future, invite feedback. And remember the 90/10 rule. That final 10 percent is crucial information—look for it and welcome it! It can be one of your greatest sources of personal growth, but hearing it takes trust, courage, and the smart person to encourage that information!

The only thing standing in the way of 100 percent disclosure is fear. Fear can be both pervasive and poisonous and is antithetical to the best qualities of human nature. Candid and honest information you get from others can be hurtful because you often see yourself differently than others do. But after you get over the initial shock, you will have a much more realistic picture of how you come off to other people. This information will be invaluable to getting to where you truly want to go.

Accountability energizes behavior

In the previous chapter the NYSE's Catherine Kinney provided an excellent example of learning to accept feedback. Doing so is a strength, not a weakness. It takes courage to allow others to participate in your journey. Sometimes the feedback reveals a needed course correction. Whenever a rocket is launched into space, reams of feedback come streaming to Earth for the duration of the flight. That feedback is not meant to hinder the journey. It's meant to keep the rocket on the right path to accomplish its objectives. In the same way feedback keeps you on course and makes you accountable.

Several years ago Bob served as a consultant to help reduce accidents in the coal mines of West Virginia. His focus was on reducing the severity and frequency of accidents. In the mines we were told that it was the safety engineer who was accountable for accidents. We saw that for accidents to be reduced we needed to help shift the accountability to the first-line supervisors and the miners. Accountability has to be in the hands of those responsible. When the foreman and the miners took this responsibility seriously, major change began to happen. Accountability energized their behavior.

You are only as accountable as you want to be. For example, knowing that you have a workout buddy energizes you to get out of bed early in the morning and go to the gym. Without that accountability partner it would be much easier to roll over and grab another hour of sleep. Accountability provides the energy to move against counterproductive behavior.

Surrounding yourself with good people

James Kennedy was the eighth director of NASA's Kennedy Space Center in Florida. He has received numerous awards, including the National Space Club's Astronautics Engineer of the Year Award and, most recently, NASA's Outstanding Leadership Medal. For Jim leadership is all about being honest. "To me truth is the ability to express your true feelings as you understand a situation—to be able to articulate it in such a way that it is what you believe to be the truth. To be successful you must be receptive—you must listen and learn. The people around you must be able to tell you what they think. This is powerful because you are tapping into hearts and minds that possess information you don't."

Prior to the loss of space shuttle *Columbia* and its seven crew members, the corporate culture within NASA made many employees feel uncomfortable expressing their opinions when they differed from management's. Jim says, "We can make it hard for others to tell us the truth. Sincere efforts are being made to promote a culture that fully encourages all opinions from all people. We need to foster a culture of open expression of opinion as well as diversity of opinions. This leads to feedback, and the backbone of feedback is truth telling. People should have the self-assured feeling that 'they do want to know what I think. It's OK to disagree.' An environment in which people feel totally comfortable expressing the truth as they know it in open and honest dialogue, knowing that their opinion on a subject may be totally different from the boss's, and it's OK. Being surrounded by people who will tell you the honest truth is a great personal asset. It keeps me on a personal growth path that wouldn't exist if I only allowed or encouraged comments that made me feel better for the time being."

NASA had drifted from a culture with a mission to a culture of survival, Jim says. "The insight that came from the *Columbia* Accident Investigation Board was that if you were not the senior person, your opinion was really not wanted. The report further cited that the real reason we lost *Columbia* was because the culture did not allow its people to tell the truth of what they saw. They saw flight films of *Columbia's* ascent and thought the shuttle might have taken a hit to the wing's leading edge, and it scared them. A culture that assumes there are no blind spots will subtly sabotage honest insights if they differ from the status quo. I know in my personal and professional life I don't feel good making a decision on virtually any subject until I've had some open, honest discussion about what my colleagues think."

What are the barriers to honest feedback? "It's one thing to say you want people to be honest," Jim says. "It's another thing to assist the process." According to Jim, some approaches can bridge desire and reality. "You encourage honesty by your behavior. It only takes a time or two for you to say, 'I want your honest opinion,' but then you slap them down or make them feel uncomfortable and insignificant. You lose credibility, and people will not feel they can tell you what they are thinking. Who loses? I do. You typically get the kind of behavior you reward."

The grass is always greener—where you water it

Your relationships impact the way you think, live, and act. When you ask, "Who are my allies and how can they help?" you are building up incredible value in your life. You've heard it said: "The grass is always greener on the other side of the fence." The truth? The grass is always greener where you water it—where you put your time and effort. Those most important relationships in your life need your time and attention. The quality of your life will be in direct proportion to the types of relationships you choose to build.

What deposits are you making right now to increase your emotional and relational holdings for the future? What you invest now will pay off big dividends when you need it the most. As Walt Disney once said, "Whatever we have accomplished has been because other people have helped us."

Touched by an angel

It's a Wonderful Life has become an all-time Christmas classic. It's a beautiful story about the priceless value of relationships. Jimmy Stewart's George Bailey is a man who has done so much for so many. He has invested in the lives of people—so much so that he sacrificed travel and adventure to do it. His father had died suddenly and he took on the responsibility of the family business. The town needed him as president of the savings and loan.

During the film we get to know George from his head to his heart. We see how he was shaped in his younger years from a boy through adolescence to become a husband, father, and business owner. His humanity and humanitarianism are magnetic. His interests always seem to take a backseat to the needs of others. But as his frustration mounts, you see it in his moods. His self-talk becomes more negative by the moment, yet he doesn't realize it. He feels stuck in his little town of Bedford Falls when he assumes the rest of the world has so much to offer. His work hours are long and tedious; other people pull on his coat, looking for him to solve their problems. And what does he get? His salary is modest, and he's living in a humble house in desperate need of repair.

When bankruptcy threatens the business, he reaches the edge of a nervous breakdown. Frustration reaches its peak. He decides to end it all on a bridge in the dead of winter, ready to throw himself into the dark, cold waters below.

But Clarence, his guardian angel, embodied as a lovable, befuddled old man, jumps first, using George's predilection for helping others to save Clarence and in so doing save himself. Through a series of supernatural events, the angel offers George perspective—to see what the lives of others would be like without him. And in that perspective George comes to realize that his life is indeed worth living. Even with his troubles his life is wonderful. George comes to his senses, his gratitude is renewed, and he goes back home to rediscover the ones he loves.

George arrives home only to discover that all those relational deposits he's made over the years have come back in an outpouring of generosity and support for him. His friends, neighbors, and business associates have taken up a collection that secures his business and saves his future. Then George discovers a note left behind by his guardian angel: "Remember, George: No man is a failure who has friends."

For Reflection

Surrounding yourself with good people, friends, or mentors takes a discerning eye, and it requires trust. To gain the trust of others, you must yourself be worthy of their trust. Build a strong group of mutual supporters by asking these questions:

1. Who are the allies I can rely on for help? How can they help me accomplish my goals?

2. What resources do I need to accomplish my goals?

3. What is my system for exposing my blind spots that slow my progress?

4. Do I keep track of what I'm saying to myself? What's the pattern of my self-talk?

5. Do I have the right people on my team? Or the wrong people? What should I do next?

6. What people are crucial to my success? Are they on my team?

Chapter 7

Knowing Who You Are and Having What You Want

We don't see things as they are; we see
them as we are.

Anais Nin

"*D*ad, you're so intense. You're
always on the edge of your seat, and no matter what I do, it isn't
good enough or fast enough. If I didn't see you act this same way
with Janie, who is practically perfect, I'd think I was totally incompetent." Stuart, a successful businessman, was taken aback by his
nervous son's vulnerable earnestness.

Instead of the usual "How dare you talk to me that way, I'm your father!" rebuke that had become his typical response to any criticism, Stuart was oddly subdued, watching his son Dave's expressions as the teenager struggled with his words. "Son, can you tell me more about that?" He listened to his son describe his experiences; it made him cringe. As he listened he remembered feeling the same way at times with his own father and how he had vowed to be a different dad when he grew up. "I had no idea I was affecting you this way. I've been so stressed at work that I've been kind of moody lately. Maybe longer than just lately from what you've just said. But that's an excuse—not an apology. Here I thought I was doing a pretty good job of keeping things to myself. I'm very sorry I've been so hard on you guys. I wanted to make sure you're trying your best, but what I was saying and how I said it could never motivate you, or anyone else for that matter. In fact all I really did was dismiss your talents, your gifts, and your abilities."

"Dad," Dave went on, "Janie and I thought you were mad at us! We were wondering what we could've done to get you so upset. We even flipped a coin to see who would ask you. I lost. It's taken me three hours of Janie's nagging for me to get up the guts to talk to you."

"Do I really come across that heavy and abrasive?"

Dave nodded. "Yes, and not only with us. You lash out at a lot of people—even people in stores and restaurants, or traffic. And I'm not the only one afraid to talk to you when you're like that."

His son's words hit Stuart squarely between his eyes as he recalled his behavior at breakfast that morning. He didn't speak to anyone at the table; instead he read the paper. Something in the news had reminded him to call his project manager, and then he flew into a tirade when he realized an important detail had fallen through the cracks. In retrospect he admitted to himself that his behavior wasn't merely rude; it was bordering on ridiculousness or madness. As much as Stuart didn't enjoy hearing about this, especially from his son, he said, "Dave, I apologize for taking my frustrations out on you, Janie, and your mom—when you are the very people that mean the most to me. I love you and don't want to repeat that type of behavior. Thank you for stepping up to the plate and allowing me to see myself as others see me."

Stuart apologized to his wife, Doris, and their daughter, Janie. Their initial reaction was immediate, positive, and forgiving. Later that evening the family went to a local restaurant. During dinner Janie, caught up in a discussion of being truthful regardless of the consequences, suddenly said, "I confess! That coin I flipped had two heads. Sorry, Dave. I'm not as gutsy as you, and I didn't want to take any chances."

Shaken again by his daughter's revelation of the fear he instilled in his household, Stuart asked, "Am I really that bad?" They all nodded.

Stuart looked at his wife, and it was like seeing the fresh-faced, smiling girl he loved from the very start. His eyes brimmed with tears as he asked, "How do you put up with me?"

Doris returned his look, thinking how the time had passed so quickly. "There have been times when it's felt like years, but more often it seems like it's been minutes."

They were silent until the waitress brought the menu and they ordered dessert. "If I've been acting like this at home without realizing it, then I must be that way at work too," said Stuart.

Doris looked up and said, "We can't answer that, but your partner, Jack, and your assistant, Pamela, can. Why don't you ask them?"

In the office

The next day Stuart approached his colleagues. His partner, Jack, replied, "I've known you a long time—you've always been intense. I thought you might be having some problems at home. Of course lately our deals with all their ups and downs would make most people nuts."

"You're my partner, so my problems are half yours. How do you keep things under control?" asked Stuart.

Jack paused for a moment before he answered. "About 10 years ago I went to a 48-hour retreat and learned about four questions that I ask myself whenever things go haywire or out of whack. Or sometimes when I just want to keep myself balanced. Answering these questions has been working for me ever since."

Jack handed Stuart a card from his wallet.

"Here, take this," he said. It was a list of four questions. "However to get the full benefit, I recommend you take a weekend retreat by yourself and do a little soul-searching and reflecting. I never used to think I had the time, but it was the best 48 hours I ever spent. You'll come back a new man, Stuart. I guarantee it."

Stuart read the card:

Who are you and what do you want?
Where are you and why are you there?
What will you do and how will you do it?
Who are your allies and how can they help?

Stuart reviewed the questions a second time and asked jokingly, "You mean you've been asking yourself these questions all these years, and you're still my partner?"

"Yup!" Jack said with a laugh.

"Do you mind if I ask you why?"

"Well, Stuart, you may fly off the handle once in a while, but I've never met a more honest person than you. You don't lie, never try to cook the books, you pay your taxes, sometimes you're so truthful people would like to put a muzzle on you. Besides, Stuart,

I trust you like my brother. And who breaks up a partnership with his trusted brother?"

"Why didn't you tell me about my behavior sooner?"

"Ask yourself how open and receptive you might have been, and you'll answer your own question."

"I see your point. I've heard the phrase 'When the student is ready, the teacher appears,'" Stuart said, leaving to speak with his assistant, Pamela. By the end of his conversation in which he shared how he planned to change, Pamela said, "Good. Now I don't have to count the days until my next vacation—or yours! Let's get you scheduled for your retreat—right now!"

Stuart went to Jack's cabin on a lake about an hour away. He brought several picture albums from his youth, his wedding, and family albums with Doris and the kids and his laptop and a camera. He hadn't looked at any of those pictures in years. At first, sitting alone on the front porch it felt strange to be all by himself. But then he reveled in things that he had never noticed before: the noise the leaves made as the breeze came from the lake, the lapping of the water on the shore, the sound of the birds on the roof, the muffled voices from fishing boats in the distance making their way across the lake.

He took the four questions card from his shirt pocket. Then he unfolded the retreat questions that Jack had given him during a long lunch when Jack told him about the process. At first he thought it was a little weird that Jack had recommended he take a picture of himself before he began, but he picked up the camera, held it at arm's length, and snapped his picture.

Stuart read through the opening exercises and remembered some of the recommendations Jack had made over lunch, comments that showed him the value of reviewing his past, reflecting, and looking openly and honestly at his earlier experiences, habits, behavior, attitudes, and beliefs. He opened his laptop and was surprised how incidents he thought he had long forgotten came to mind as he wrote. Later while reviewing his notes, he began to notice that his need to be both perfect and right and his failure to fulfill those needs were the source of his anger and frustration, having nothing to do with any business deals themselves. That led him to consider ways of altering his behavior. Instead of debating others and acting like he had to prove himself in a business or personal situation, he thought, he would begin asking people, "What do you think about this?" Just that one shift already made him feel more relaxed. He spent the rest of the day working through the exercises, stopping only to enjoy the picnic lunch and dinner he brought along.

Sitting outside the cabin having breakfast the next morning overlooking the lake, he watched some boys sailing. Their laughter jostled old memories of fishing with his dad in Idaho and a weekend river trip they once took together. He resolved to take his own son and daughter on one-on-one trips so that he could really get to know them, to learn how they thought about themselves and their own futures. He realized that while he was doing this weekend retreat to find out about himself, the greater joy would be sharing what he learned with his kids and helping them discover who they are and what they want in their own life journeys. By the end of the second day, Stuart felt more relaxed than he had in years, maybe ever. As he was picking up after himself, he realized how grateful he was that the cabin was out of cell phone range and that Jack's family didn't have a television. There had been nothing to distract him for two full days. Next year, he told himself, he could have his retreat anywhere or anytime because he was confident he now knew what to do and how to do it. He could now quiet his mind and be calm because he now had the skills to do so. He then snapped another picture of himself and compared the two. "Two different people," he thought to himself. One looked stressed and the other actually looked younger and more relaxed.

The results didn't end there. Afterward he immediately started to enjoy learning what other people thought at work and at parties and from the person sitting next to him on a plane. He learned new things and insights he had never known about or explored before and heard points of view he never would have considered. He began to enjoy all his time with his family instead of just a few hours on the weekend or randomly during the week. His relationship with his family and partner flourished like never before, and the people with whom he did business seemed buoyed by his new enthusiasm and passion for his work. He began to value his time and realized it was his most valuable commodity. His curiosity and honesty made his everyday interactions nurturing, uplifting, and happy, no matter whom they were with or what they were about. He enjoyed himself. It was as if the pace of his life slowed down, yet he was getting more things done and more effectively than ever before. He reviewed his notes from his retreat on a regular basis, adding new insights as they occurred.

He realized that for the first time people were going out of their way to help him. "Is there anything I can do to help? Are you looking for something? Let me order that for you; it'll make working on those plans so much easier. I have a wonderful table for you and your party right now; come this way" were things he heard on a daily basis. To Stuart it was as if people were a little more interesting than they had been before. And that's true—but only because Stuart was a lot more interesting and much more interested.

Build strong personal relationships

Strong personal relationships not only make the journey to the best of your life possible, they make it more enjoyable. They yield great rewards, but they also take a sense of engagement to establish, flourish, and keep. Building strong relationships with friends, spouses, family, coworkers, and others requires intimacy by being open and vulnerable with them. Being open and vulnerable requires trust, and by now you know all about that subject: Successful relationships are built on your trust, and the foundation of trust is honesty, and honesty in your own life originates from only one place—you.

Can you develop intimacy with others without being truthful? The truth is—you can't. If someone doesn't trust you to be truthful, then instead of developing emotional intimacy with you, that person will close up. Vice versa, if you don't trust someone to be truthful with you, you will shut him or her out.

If you're as focused as Stuart was on work and achievement to the point that you don't keep your promises to friends and family, you are not being truthful with yourself or your family. Better to be honest and admit that in reality and in practice your family is less important to you than to lie to yourself and to them. The game is over—everyone knows how you feel even if it hasn't been expressed openly by you or them.

People can deal with the truth more easily than with a lie that's never exposed. For example when kids recognize a disconnect between what their parents say and what they do, it can set in motion a lasting downward spiral of family dysfunction that can last for decades, even for a lifetime. That spiral, however, can be cut short when a father with an attitude like Stuart's can say, "I didn't know how to make you know that I love you other than to work hard to give you everything you deserve, so please bear with me. I want to change. Maybe if we can all work together, I'll learn other ways to show you that you mean the world to me." Or a mother who can say, "I've been so busy trying to take care of everything that in the end I haven't taken care of you or me. Let's help each other connect the disconnect. Let's see how we can all help each other to be who we are and achieve what we want—and plan it together."

"Buy the truth and do not sell it; get wisdom, discipline, and understanding." Those aren't our words—it's wisdom written thousands of years ago, Proverbs 23:23. If you are willing to commit yourself 100 percent to the truth and hold on to it, even when the temptation to let it go is strong, you're going to gain wisdom—the skills for living. You're going to gain discipline—the action you take to follow your good intentions. You're going to gain understanding—the ability to bring the values and goals in your life together in meaningful ways that provide a picture of the future. Building strong personal relationships requires a personal commitment to seek the truth and, once it's found, to build on it.

Speak the truth—always?

There are hundreds of ways you can justify something less than the whole truth. You may want to avoid decisions, to be concerned about hurting another's feelings or welfare, to delay change. Obscuring the truth, however, inevitably results in far more problems than it avoids.

But does that mean you should always tell all of the truth to everyone? For example if you have negative information regarding a close friend that would be hurtful if he or she heard it, should you share it? The answer to this question depends completely on your intent and on the boundaries of your relationship.

What is your intent in telling that person the truth? Is it to hurt or to help? The biblical admonition is "speak the truth in love." Are you telling the truth for your own benefit or for the benefit of the other person? When you give feedback are you giving it because you want to help, or are you using it as a weapon to hurt someone?

When it comes time to speak, examine your own intent; hold your own counsel. How you disseminate the truth and your motivations need to be considered carefully. While what you have to say might be absolutely true, if it's not spoken "in love," if it's not offered entirely for the other person's benefit, don't speak. For instance do adults tell children when they are growing up the entire truth about everything (tooth fairy included!)? No, adults tell them what they need to know, what they can understand, for their good. As they grow and mature, their ability to handle the truth increases, and their parents, teachers, and others can provide more truth. In the context of personal relationships, truth telling is to be provided at a level that person can take. This involves making a judgment. It's the wise person who can distinguish what to say, to whom, and when.

Helping others with the truth

Some years ago Mick visited Haiti to work with people in several clinics. At one stop during his travels around the island, he saw a farmer working a field with a donkey and plow. Nearby sat a used tractor. Mick asked the director of the clinic, "Why don't you teach him how to use the tractor?"

The director explained, "That's too big a leap from what he knows now. We have to go one step at a time. That will change, but for today asking him to drive that tractor would be as insensitive as asking one of your great-great-grandparents to fire up your computer and shop for Christmas presents on Amazon.com." It was not a matter of intelligence; it was a matter of that farmer having an entirely different worldview. So from the farmer's perspective, what would be more helpful? Sometimes you have to offer the truth in digestible pieces, carefully matched to the person's ability to receive it, understand it, and apply it. That is speaking the truth in love.

When you have bad news for someone, consider the following before you speak: What is my motive? Is my intention to help this person? Or am I trying to convince myself that I'm being virtuous by telling the truth, knowing full well it's not in that person's best interest?

Consider this example: Sally wants to tell a coworker point-blank that other people think badly of him, that they think he's inconsiderate and aggressive. Does she tell herself that she's doing this "because he needs to know the truth" when she really wants to put him in his place? Or is Sally's motivation for providing her coworker with this feedback to help him change his behavior before he is fired or passed over for a promotion? If so, that feedback—that truth—could be given "in love." Sally must develop a motivation of caring, to offer provision or protection, before she delivers the truth to another.

Truth both provides and protects. If you use it in a way other than to create provision or protection—to harm or to disillusion—then you should hold your tongue. Examine your motivations before speaking.

Being transparent and vulnerable

Building strong, long-lasting relationships requires taking them to a deeper level of truth. That's where the real growth takes place. Building relationships requires speaking the truth to others, and it requires accepting the truth from others. You make yourself transparent and vulnerable to receive it from others.

Mick can offer an example from his own family: When our son was starting ninth grade, my wife, Louise, and I sat him down and in so many words told him, "Mark, we all have similar goals. You want to be free. Our goal for you is we want you to be free. Now along the way we're going to have some tensions. You will think you should be free sooner, and we will think you should not be as free as you already are at that time. So we're all coming at the issue of your freedom from different viewpoints and with a bit of a delayed response.

"A delayed response is inevitable in life and in relationships. Oftentimes we make a decision and have to wait a while to see the result. It's like adjusting the shower between hot and cold; we turn the knob but there's a delay until the water comes out at the new temperature. We tend to overcorrect one direction or the other, and then we have to adjust again. That happens in relationships too, but we can't let it hijack our relationship. When we do have that tension—because we don't think you should be that free, and you think you should be more free—remember that we're all on the same page. Our goal is for you to be free!"

Throughout the four years Mark was in high school, there were times when he would come to his mother and me and push back and say, "I think you're being unreasonable" or "I think you're too strict."

Often we would say to him, "You know what, Mark? You're absolutely right."

We'd get into a discussion about why I reacted a certain way, and usually I'd find that it was from my own experience growing up and that my own upbringing was causing me to overprotect as a parent. And many times during our discussions, I would see my son's jaw drop because I admitted a frailty, or agreed that he was right and I was off base, or confessed I'd made an incorrect assumption. It feels great when your child comes back later and says he or she has adopted some of your thought processes and they work.

Recognizing your own mistakes and the fact that you are learning, admitting your vulnerability, and acting with transparency will increase cooperation exponentially. Most parents don't tell their kids that they have taught their parents an important lesson. Nor do most spouses tell each other, nor do employers tell their employees. But they all should. In the office when employees figure out that the boss is "always right" and can't be taught, the relationship petrifies. But when a boss is open to learning, interpersonal relationships are made stronger, more meaningful, more enduring, and more profitable as employees buy into the mission.

Building relational equity

Everyone knows that building a financial equity portfolio increases your wealth. Your deposits multiply, and the total value grows. It's important to also know that the same is true in your relationships—in fact even more so. Build a relational equity portfolio and you can draw on it throughout your life. Your relationships impact the way you think, live, and act. During tough times if your portfolio is full, you'll have a cushion. If it is empty, you'll find yourself continually fixing short-term relationships, where the names are different but the problems are familiar. Serial relationships are for people who don't know how to add value to relationships. The secret to adding value to your relationship portfolio is this: You don't grow a relationship by taking; you grow it by giving.

In their book *Just Enough: Tools for Creating Success in Your Work and Life*, authors Laura Nash and Howard Stevenson define enduring success as "...a collection of activities that are viewed affirmatively by you and those you care about—now, throughout your life, and beyond."[1] Ask yourself: What are the things that you and those close to you most care about? When someday you find yourself on your deathbed, thinking back over your life, what will you ask for? We've never once heard anyone say, "Would you please bring my awards, my trophies, and my medals? I want to see them one more time." You won't want to be surrounded by trophies and other material junk; you'll want to be surrounded by those who care most about you and whom you care about. Are these people you love and trust and cherish a part of your definition of success? If not, you need to be truthful and define what success really is for you. And you need to do it sooner—not later. You can't choose the date, place, and time you meet your Maker, but you can choose to be prepared for the time when it comes. Make your deposits on a daily basis that will build your relational equity portfolio. Bring great meaning to your life now, throughout your life, and beyond.

> Make your deposits on a daily basis that will build your relational equity portfolio— bringing meaning to your life now, throughout your life, and beyond.

The impact you have on others is significant. How you behave with another person—whether it's your spouse, partner, team member, child, neighbor, or the coffee server who made your latte this morning—is an extension of who you really are and demonstrates that you know who you are and what you want. The impact you make on people, whether it's money you give, actions you take, or the way you make them feel, is what provides meaning. Think of the impact you've had on every person you interact with, because how you behave with them should be an extension of who you are.

Are you ready to begin your journey to the best of your life?

It's easy to lose sight of your destination. There are countless options available, countless turns, unexpected detours that can take you toward or away from where you want to go. Combine that with the breakneck speed of 21st-century life and it's easy to lose our bearings and get lost. It's easy to panic and start frantically looking for some familiar territory, going full throttle, hoping something pops up that looks familiar.

Four-Dimensional Thinking is your personal global positioning system, providing perspective, vision, clarity, transparency, and direction. You may feel stuck. You may face a confusing array of options. You may feel as if things are moving too fast or you need an antidote against complacency. You may feel life has been reduced to a series of birthdays. If so, ask yourself:

Who are you and what do you want?
Where are you and why are you there?
What will you do and how will you do it?
Who are your allies and how can they help?

Do your answers suggest that you need a change? Only you can determine that. Change is difficult for all of us. Someone once said, "Only vending machines and babies like change." On the other hand, change simply for the sake of change can feel like whiplash. What's needed in life is productive change—change that's created by redesigning your future; change that allows you to get rid of excess baggage, travel light, and keep short accounts. Change differentiates you without isolating you.

One of the benefits of knowing who you are is that you will seldom be blindsided by problems. And in the face of a crisis, you can know that nothing harmful can touch you in a permanent way. You learn to learn from your failures. They produce disequilibrium; they force you to catch your balance. They put your values to the test.

"When we connect our plans to personal meaning, we develop the endurance to handle the tough times," says Catherine Kinney, president of the New York Stock Exchange. "Clarity of what we want creates the standards that keep us moving forward when the wind is in our face." You can have confidence, flexibility, and resilience to weather the crises, the crucibles of life.

As financier Warren Buffett says, "When the tide goes out, you discover who's been swimming naked." The Four Dimensions keep us clothed, even during the low tides of life. Clarity creates hope, and people with hope don't overreact to negativism or setbacks. When you are clear on where you are going, you move straight ahead through anxiety without overreacting. Rather than being diffused by problems, your energy becomes focused like a laser.

What is your legacy?

Too many people step on the stage of life and feel that they don't know their lines. They are confused, frustrated, frightened, or embarrassed. What a confidence-building feeling it is to know the plotline—to know where the story is going! That knowledge creates excitement, a sense of anticipation, and a feeling of assurance that produces exhilaration and even joy in the midst of change. We asked Coach John Wooden on his 96th birthday why at his age he was so enthusiastic and excited about life. He replied, "The moment your past becomes more exciting than your future is the day you start to die."

Understanding who you are and what you want creates harmony in your life. Without this it's like trying to connect with music when you are tone-deaf. You can't tell whether you're in tune. So start with the goal of clarity. When you know who you are, what you want tends to show up. As Frances Hesselbein said to us, "Service to others and a passion for your own mission and work create a powerful synergy. It's about seeing how your strengths and passions align with the needs you see and are in a position to meet."

> "The moment your past becomes more exciting than your future is the day you start to die." —John Wooden

Working with PRIDE

Mike Ziegler is an individual who really understands that people can never be satisfied by more and more material things in their lives. Mike was the general manager of two large retail companies and owned another chain. He described himself as motivated and driven by making lots of money.

As Mike says, "There is nothing wrong with making lots of money, but somehow I realized that who you are is not what you have."

Mike retired and moved to the foothills of Sacramento in the early 1980s, looking for something to do. He had no idea how dramatically his life was about to change. After such a successful career managing the retail businesses and owning a car wash chain, he was prepared to enjoy family life and eventually plan his next career. Then an amazing thing happened. He was asked to visit a local non-profit organization, Placer Rehabilitation Industries. The company was started in 1966 in the basement of a church by a group of parents who had children with disabilities to provide better lives and futures for their own children. Deep down inside, a thunderbolt told Mike that this was where he was meant to be.

As he studied the company in 1983, it had a budget of $250,000 and 65 employees. His passion to do something bigger than himself took over and he joined the company. The thought of helping people with disabilities gave Mike a level of commitment and excitement he had never experienced before. By 1985 the nonprofit company, now known as PRIDE, showed revenue of $1.4 million with 241 employees; in 2006 revenue was $95.2 million with more than 3,000 employees. Today there are about 4,000 employees and revenues well in excess of $100 million.

"Blessed with the gift of gab and the life decision that brought me to PRIDE, I began what has been a 25-year labor of love," Mike says. "An entrepreneur at heart, I did everything to bring in work for our nonprofit company—from hawking wares at a local swap meet to knocking on doors of area businesses. At the root of our success was the cultivation of a can-do attitude to put people with disabilities to work and to prove it's all about ability and not disability."

Working with people with disabilities changed Mike's life and his priorities, and he continues to reflect upon doing things for a greater cause. "The longer that I work at PRIDE, the more I know that none of us have a clue to what truly happens when somebody who couldn't get a job suddenly gets a job.

"For example one of PRIDE's board members, Mike Snegg, has a friend who is a world-class cardiologist in Southern California. His son, whom we'll call Tom, has a severe disability. They couldn't get him a job, couldn't do anything, and they wanted to help him. Mike told me he owed his life to this doctor and asked if there was something we could do to help his family. I sent one of our representatives, John Oliver, to the family, even though the doctor lived out of Oliver's geographical district. PRIDE will go help whoever needs it. I got an email yesterday from Oliver that says Tom just started a job at the market. Tom was so excited he called all of his relatives. I'm paraphrasing, but the email would have brought you to your knees. We take it for granted, this stuff that you wouldn't even give a second thought. But to somebody who couldn't get a job before, getting that job was the greatest thing in the world."

Since his decision to lead PRIDE in 1983, Mike has led the company's as well as his own transformation. PRIDE has moved from an organization dependent on federal and state funds to a self-sufficient, nonprofit business enterprise providing services to Fortune 500 companies and government customers nationwide. If you reach Mike's voice-mail greeting, you will hear his joyful voice saying: "Hi, this is Mike 'lucky to be working at PRIDE' Ziegler!"

How do you define success?

What is it that's going to be of real value in your life? What do you want from success? What is it that's really going to challenge you? What will make a difference in the world? What will attract you? What will endure even after you've moved on?

Aristotle noted that happiness was composed of many desired ends, not just one. People go mad seeking success, and many go even madder once they possess it.

Lily was 93 years old and weakening. She knew she was headed into her final days.

"Tell my grandchildren," she said to her son, "to enjoy every day! There's no reason not to make each day into something you can enjoy. When you get where I am right now, all the things you worried about, all the problems you thought you had will seem very mundane or silly and a waste of your precious time. And tell my children—your brothers and sister—to enjoy themselves and their children—my grandchildren. When people can't laugh or smile, it means they're not enjoying their lives. I sure did, but now that I think back ..." she paused, then laughed and continued. "Come to think of it, I could have enjoyed myself even more than I did!"

Your personal journey for the best of your life has many possible destinations. Enjoy every trip, every new start, every detour, and every arrival. Enjoy all the people you meet; they are with you because they trust you and the direction you're going. After all, you are in command of your journey! You are the one who moves your life from good to better to best!

For Reflection

This chapter explored the impact of truthfulness on personal relationships. You must have truth in your life to develop long-term, meaningful relationships, both within yourself and with others. To build stronger personal relationships, ask yourself the following questions:

1. How do I take care of my personal relationships?

2. When in conversation with others, am I trying to prove my point or listen to others?

3. How do I envision my legacy?

4. Do I speak the truth in love? To whom? Has there ever been a time when I spoke the truth but not in love? What happened? How did I feel afterwards? How did I make the other person feel?

Chapter 8

Your 48-Hour Personal Retreat

What lies behind you and what lies before you are tiny matters when compared to what lies within you.

Ralph Waldo Emerson

*T*here is no better way to design a better future for yourself, your family, and your career than taking a day—preferably two—away from your usual routine to reflect on who you are and what you want.

Clients who have used our *Who Am I and What Do I Want?* Personal Retreat either privately or in corporate retreat settings say it has been the most valuable time they've experienced for many years. They tell us that they were surprised how the private time they set aside to reflect on their lives affected them on a deep level and made it much easier for them to put into place action plans that have moved them toward what they want in life. Many have made it an annual event to refresh and renew the length and breadth of their personal and work lives and make adjustments to calibrate their lives. Continual renewal ensures long-lasting enjoyment of what will become the best of your life!

This chapter serves as your catalyst for planning what is appropriate to you and the life you want to lead. What follows is an outline of exercises designed to assist you in thinking about your life using the Four Dimensions we describe in this book. Use these exercises to guide you through your own reflective journey. By the end of your retreat you won't have any hesitation in answering the question, *Who are you and what do you want?*

Preparation for the retreat

Your personal retreat is exactly that—personal. It is important that you spend time alone. Urge others to support you.

No worthwhile retreat happens without preparation. Start by arranging to go somewhere special—a quiet place where you can stay alone for approximately 48 hours. It might be a mountain retreat; a tent in a quiet campsite; somewhere by the beach, lake, or desert; or just a favorite place where you are comfortable and won't be interrupted by a television, cell phone, email, or PDA.

Plan ahead for healthy meals and snacks, health, hygiene, and medical necessities. Bring comfortable clothes appropriate to your chosen destination. Fresh air and a little activity will help stimulate your thinking. You may want to take walks in the woods or on the beach, hike in mountains, or go swimming. Check the weather forecast to be prepared.

You will find it useful to bring the following items for your personal retreat:

Pens or pencils, pencil sharpener
Notebook or journal
Scissors
Glue stick
Small poster board
Handful of colored markers or pencils
Pictures, school yearbooks, photo albums, and other memorabilia from different stages of your life and significant events (childhood, adolescence, young adulthood, weddings, birthdays, anniversaries, etc.)
Camera

During the retreat progress at your own pace. The exercises are designed to build upon one another, leading you through a reflective personal journey. We have provided space on the following pages to write your thoughts, truths, concerns, ideas, desires, hopes, realities, and dreams. Write your comments on the pages or photocopy them and collect your finished pages in a folder or a binder to review in a few months. We encourage you to use a journal, laptop computer, or notebook to record your thoughts apart from the exercises. You will remember things from your life you thought were long forgotten, but now they will hold new meaning. Write whatever comes to mind; allow your imagination to venture far past its present boundaries. That alone will make this experience unique, creative, and meaningful.

Beginning your retreat

Once you arrive at your quiet place, unpack and settle into your workspace. Breathe in deeply and exhale slowly a few times until you are feeling relaxed. Take a picture of yourself before you begin. Now take a few pictures of the setting you have chosen indoors and out. Your photos can serve as a reminder of your retreat during the months and years that follow. Preview the exercises that follow. The questions are straightforward, designed to build on one another, but if you don't have an answer right away, feel free to put a question or two aside and return to them later. Or review the section of the book or your "For Reflection" notes to which the question refers. You are in complete control of your retreat!

EXERCISE 1

List below or on a piece of paper all the roles you currently play in life (for example: mother, son, boss, housekeeper, gardener, chauffeur, personal event planner, financial investor, role model, babysitter, nurse, confidant, psychologist, neighbor, friend, grandparent, aunt or uncle, etc.). Your answers will help take you to the core of who you are—your personal talents, passions, and obligations.

From the list you have created, select four roles that are the most important to you at this stage of your life.

1.

2.

3.

4.

Write out these thoughts for each role. Space is provided on the following pages, or write in your retreat journal.

Example: Role: Parent

What I believe others expect of me regarding this role	What I expect of myself regarding this role
provide emotional support for my children	understand my children's needs
face any conflict with my kids, teachers, or school ASAP	take time to understand my children's talents and potential
create a wholesome and enjoyable environment in our home	help my kids develop their interests even though they may be nothing like mine
take care of my children's health care and education	share concerns and discuss family decisions with my spouse and agree to present a united front with our children
attend their sports, recitals, and school events	never criticize them publicly
make birthdays and holidays a priority	plan time with kids on weekends and vacations during school breaks
pay our bills	listen, really listen

Role #1: _____

What I believe others expect of me regarding this role	What I expect of myself regarding this role

Role #2: _____

What I believe others expect of me regarding this role	What I expect of myself regarding this role

Role #3: _____

What I believe others expect of me regarding this role	What I expect of myself regarding this role

Role #4: _____

What I believe others expect of me regarding this role

What I expect of myself regarding this role

What you have just described can bring definition, boundaries, joy, and fulfillment to what you're experiencing now or your plans for the future. The key to the best of your life is developing and maintaining healthy relationships. The Interdependence Model described and diagrammed on the following pages will help you examine the types of relationships you have right now. As we explained in Chapter 6, two forces in your life are in constant ebb and flow: the force for togetherness and the force for separateness. Too much separateness can lead to an unhealthy independence, while too much togetherness can result in an unhealthy dependence. These forces stand in dynamic tension, pulling you in one direction or the other. Interdependence is an acquired balance between the two. It's something you learn to do; it rarely comes naturally.

Refer back to each of the four roles you described. Write the name of the person you primarily relate to in each role. Do you have a sense of interdependence with that person?

Once you see on paper your own relationship formulas—the patterns of how you interact with others—you can make better choices about your time, energy, and sense of engagement. Having a balanced life means your relationships with others are more enjoyable because you are more enthusiastically engaged. You are a magnet for other balanced people.

Altering any relationship takes thinking, patience, time, and focus. How might you develop interdependence in all your relationships? Interdependence in any relationship begins with you. If you behave interdependently you become the model for others close to you to follow. If you take the lead, the dance begins.

The Interdependence Model

To measure the dynamics of separateness and togetherness at work in each relationship, rate your agreement or disagreement with the following statements on a scale of 1 to 5 (1 means you strongly disagree; 5 means you strongly agree):

☐ I don't really care about what others think.

☐ I seldom ask others for help.

☐ My preference is to work alone.

☐ Total Independent

☐ I value other people's opinions more than my own.

☐ When others get angry with me, I blame myself.

☐ I find it difficult to stand up for myself.

☐ Total Dependent

☐ I find myself being oversensitive to other people's needs.

☐ I feel better about myself when people need me.

☐ I function better when someone is dependent on me.

☐ Total Codependent

☐ I think it is important for the people in my life to have their own space.

☐ I am able to share my opinion with others without fear of losing the relationship.

☐ If I take someone's advice, I don't blame that person if it doesn't work out.

☐ Total Interdependent

Place each total in the appropriate box on the following page.

Separateness–Measures your need for autonomy
Togetherness–Measures your need for connectivity

The Interdependence Model

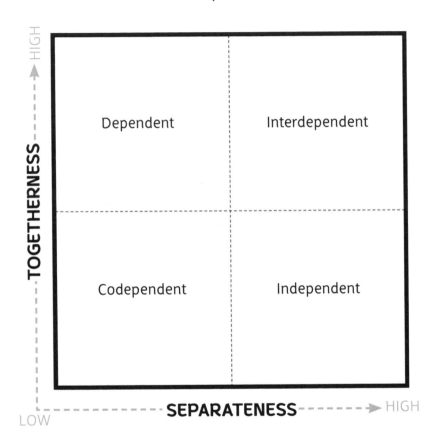

What do your scores mean? If you scored 1 to 5 in any of the cat-
egories, it is not your primary way of interacting in a relationship.
If you scored from 6 to 10 in any category, it may be your secondary way of interacting. If you scored from 11 to 15 in any category,
it is likely your primary way of interacting in a relationship.

The following descriptions explain how you relate to others. (For more on the Interdependence Model, see Chapter 6.)

Dependent: In this kind of relationship you constantly defer to others to make decisions for you. Your identity is tied to the way others feel about and react to you. What people say or don't say to you or about you can make or break your day. The danger in this is that your life slowly and often imperceptably is taken over by others..

Independent: You prefer acting alone. You may appear to be inattentive to others and at worst self-absorbed when that may not be your intention. The danger is that you isolate yourself from others, making intimate relationships more difficult.

Codependent: Your sense of self is defined by your relationship with others. There are no boundaries between your true self and others. It is difficult for you to say "no"; you put yourself last. You also attempt to control others by taking responsibility for them. You often find yourself in tightly tangled relationships.

Interdependent: In this model there is a healthy balance between yourself and others. You are able to differentiate where you end and others begin. You take responsibility and ownership for your own actions and at the same time are influenced and affected by others. You recognize your need to interact with others without depending on their changing moods to shape who you are.

Reflection

Identify the roles you play and the relationships that are critical to those roles. Are you controlling or being controlled? Do you have a healthy balance between receiving and giving in your relationships? In what ways would you like to maintain or change how you relate to others? What relationships are most precious to you? How would you like those relationships to look in the future?

EXERCISE 2

Imagine a path that stretches from the beginning of your life to where you are today. We call that a lifeline, and in this exercise you will illustrate your lifeline.

Your lifeline can help you review your past—where you came from—and determine where you are now. Have you taken yourself for granted in the past? How does your life now compare to the life you had growing up? It is critical to see where you have come from to do a better job planning your future.

Take a large piece of paper or poster board on which to draw your path. Your line can look like a road, a path through the woods, a shoreline, a sidewalk, or a simple line. It can be as plain or creative or crazy as you like. As you draw your lifeline, fill in significant details of your life so far. At the start write your birth date and at the end today's date. Along the path list every significant event, celebration, birth, death, disappointment, education and career advancement, relationship, accomplishment, time of hardship, sadness, or peak experience. Mark the times you were so happy you cried or broke out into song, and the times your tears came from sorrow. Use marking pens, crayons, ink, or pastels—anything that will make it fun for you.

Don't worry about your artistic ability; just let yourself go. As you work you'll remember events, significant relationships, and what happened with them. Write every event as it occurs to you, big or small.

Here are some questions to help you put together your lifeline. If possible write the date of each event or episode.

What were the peak experiences in your life—the ones filled with emotion, such as your graduation, your wedding, or your first child graduating from high school? Spend some time reliving those experiences. When did they happen? How did you feel? Did you laugh? Did you celebrate? Visualize the experiences from beginning to end. What was it about each experience that made it significant for you? Make a list of all the strengths, skills, talents, abilities, and resources you used in your peak experiences. Who was with you? Where were you?

Here's some other questions to help you look back:
What were the most emotional times in your life?
What made the difference between feeling down or feeling great?
What were you most interested in while growing up?
Who were the people who had the most influence in your life?
What were some of your major decisions?
What were the highlights in grammar school, middle school, high school, and college? What were the lowlights?
What were some of the biggest changes that happened to you?
When were you most successful?
When did you feel like a failure?
Whom did you love? And who loved you?
What were your most significant work experiences?
What were your most significant family experiences?

EXERCISE 3

What I believe to be my strengths	What I believe to be areas I need to improve

What do I perceive that other people think are my strengths?

What do I believe that other people think are my weaknesses?

What are the obstacles that get in the way of my being successful?

Is there anything that is difficult for me to admit about myself?

What are the top three areas in which I would like to improve?

Make a note to call or email a close friend or family member once you return home and ask him or her what he or she sees as your strengths as well as areas you need to improve. Does the person say anything different than what you recorded during your retreat? If so, why do you suppose that is? If he or she echoes what you have said, you have already learned or have begun to learn to see yourself as others see you.

EXERCISE 4

Fill in the Discovering Who I Am grid (refer to Chapter 6 for a description of the four quadrants). Think carefully about your answers. Be truthful with yourself.

Discovering Who I Am

Open and Authentic	My Blind Spots
What I know about myself and allow others to know about me	What others see in me but I don't or can't see about myself
My Secret Self	**My Hidden Potential**
What I know about myself that others don't know about me	What others don't see in me and I don't yet know about myself

What do I value?

What is important to me? What do I value most in my life?

What do I believe?

What do I believe? Write a series of one-sentence belief statements.

Example: *I believe in forgiveness.*

EXERCISE 5

Self-talk

Self-talk is the dialogue that goes on inside your head when faced with conflict, life challenges, or even simple day-to-day concerns. This aspect of yourself engages in a running commentary about everything you do. It never lets anything go by without some comment, remark, or evaluation.

You may recognize some of the following thoughts because you may have heard them all your life:

I'm not smart enough.

Something is wrong.

I can't do it.

I never finish anything.

This is too hard.

Change takes too long.

People will never love and appreciate me the way I want them to.

I have to do everything around here or it won't get done.

What are they thinking about me?

If these seem like some of the negative thoughts that you experience often, you didn't invent them yesterday. These thoughts are usually formed during childhood from comments you heard from a parent, teacher, or someone in authority. Now as an adult you have incorporated them into your own personality. You don't need those people to tell you what to do anymore. They are living inside your head rent-free. It's about time to cut them loose, and you'll learn how to in the next two exercises.

Write down your lines of self-talk dialogue. What do you say to yourself throughout the day? (Leave some space after each line to add some new self-talk.)

Now move to change negative self-talk into positive, inspiring, and self-motivating self-talk:

I'm smart enough.

Something is right.

I can do it.

I always finish everything.

Everything is easy once you do it.

Change takes time, and I am patient and disciplined.

People love and appreciate me the way I want them to because now I look at things such as kindness, consideration, and appreciation as love.

I am relaxed about getting things done by doing them right the first time.

People love to help me because I make being part of my team energizing, purposeful, fulfilling, and enjoyable.

It doesn't matter what people think about me as long as I know that I am honest with myself.

Take the negative self-talk you wrote on the previous page and transform your words into positive, self-motivating, and self-inspiring self-talk. Think about the positive truths you've just written and take a walk. Think about how you will incorporate your new self-talk into your life, replacing forever the old, outdated, yesterday's newspaper way of thinking.

Now would be a good time to take a walk and think about how much stronger you feel. Take in some deep breaths and pick up your pace. If you are walking and other people are around you, observe them and ask yourself what kind of self-talk those strangers are saying to themselves. Is it negative or is it positive? How can you tell? Is it becoming more obvious to you? Later when you get back to your book, journal, or computer, record your observations.

EXERCISE 6

Describe the greatest successes in your life. Refer back to your life-line for help.

Describe your greatest failures.

What were your most significant work experiences?

What have been the most significant decisions in your life?

What do you enjoy about those decisions?

Did you get the results you wanted? What were the immediate results? What were the long-term results? How is your life better (or worse) today as a result of making those decisions?

Would you do anything differently? What lessons did you learn?

What would you repeat in a similar situation?

EXERCISE 7

Dreams
What will you do and how will you do it?

Make a list of your dreams for your life. Look as far into the future as you like and include work, family, social, and personal. Beside each dream list the realities that will help you fulfill the dream and those that might limit it. Be very specific about how these realities might favor or limit your dreams.

Below is a list of a few areas you may want to focus on during this exercise. You may pick more than one category or invent others.

Health
Lifestyle
Career
Relationships
Spirituality
Education

For each dream in each category write down where you are.
For example:

Health: *My cholesterol level is 212.*

Lifestyle: *I am living in a foreign country and I don't speak the language.*

Career: *I have been giving my job only a percentage of what I am capable of, and that is interfering with my success.*

Relationships: *My most personal relationship is not what it once was.*

Spirituality: *My beliefs and my behavior do not match.*

Education: *Others who have the kind of job I want have an M.B.A.*

For each category write down where you want to be. Get used to saying "I want …"

Example:
Health: *I want my cholesterol level to be under 200.*
Lifestyle: *I want to speak conversational German in six months.*
Career: *I want to be promoted in one year.*
Relationships: *I want to make my most personal relationship meaningful, intimate, exciting, and full of laughter.*
Spirituality: *I want to feel congruent and feel that no matter where I am, I am myself.*
Education: *I want to make applications to the schools that I want to have on my resume.*

For each category you choose, write down action steps that you believe are necessary to achieve your desired result.

Health: *Walk on treadmill at office fitness center 30 minutes three times a week.*
Lifestyle: *Purchase German language course; listen during morning drive.*
Career: *Review my performance reviews for past three years. Study position requirements for next level.*
Relationships: *Schedule an evening out with my spouse.*
Spirituality: *Schedule 10 minutes of quiet reflection at home each weekday morning.*
Education: *Check the websites of the schools; bookmark the application pages; complete one application a week.*

My life dream for Health:

Where I am:

Where I want to be:

Action steps:

My life dream for Lifestyle:

Where I am:

Where I want to be:

Action steps:

My life dream for Career:

Where I am:

Where I want to be:

Action steps:

My life dream for Relationships:

Where I am:

Where I want to be:

Action steps:

My life dream for Spirituality:

Where I am:

Where I want to be:

Action steps:

My life dream for Education:

Where I am:

Where I want to be:

Action steps:

My life dream for _____:

Where I am:

Where I want to be:

Action steps:

A practically perfect day

Nothing is ever perfect, but describe a near-perfect day for you five years from today: Where are you? Take a mental snapshot. How have you incorporated your dreams (what you wrote about in the previous section) into that day? In your perfect day who is with you? What are you doing? How do you feel? What expression is on your face? Are you worried? Smiling? Does your body feel relaxed?

EXERCISE 8

In Chapter 5 we presented a simple model for making change called Force Field Analysis. On one side of the situation are forces that help you carry out change, and on the other side are forces that hinder change. It is important to be able to identify both the forces that help you change and the forces that work against changing your life for the better. The key is to choose the forces for change and withdraw your support from those opposed to change.

Use pages 220 and 221 to create several change models for your life. Name something you want to change or improve about yourself. Then identify the forces restraining you from achieving your preferred future and the forces encouraging the change.

Force Field Analysis

Desired change in my life:

What are the forces restraining me from achieving my preferred future? List them on the right side of the diagram. On a scale of 1 to 5, label their strength. (1 is the weakest; 5 is the strongest.)

What are the forces encouraging change? List them on the left side of the diagram. On a scale of 1 to 5, label their strength. (1 is the weakest; 5 is the strongest.)

Which of my strengths can I draw on to weaken the restraining forces and strengthen the forces for change?

What additional support or advice do I need to reach my preferred future? How and when will I get that advice? Later how will I show those who support me and/or give me advice that I appreciate the help they give me?

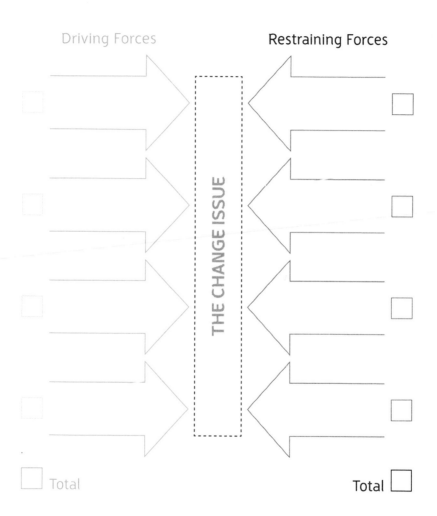

Driving Forces

Restraining Forces

THE CHANGE ISSUE

Total

Total

EXERCISE 9

Set SMART goals

Specific **M**easurable **A**ttainable **R**elevant **T**ime-bound

This exercise is a crucial part of your life improvement process. You may want to refer back to Chapter 5 to review SMART goals. While you may have written goals in the past, this time you can do it by asking yourself the questions below. Then write down your goals. Notice the difference with which you approach writing your goals after a little self-intervention:

Which aspects of my life would I like to improve?

How will I keep track of my progress? What are the best and easiest ways I can demonstrate my improvement to myself? What simple monitoring system can I use?

How can I clarify my targets or goals and make them meaningful to me? What's at stake? What deadline am I shooting for?

Who needs to know and who cares most about my progress? Are there others who can help me? What kind of feedback will be most helpful to me: my own, others', or a combination?

How am I going to maintain my improvements? How can I set up a personal means of recognition to gauge my progress? How will I celebrate my successes?

How can I evaluate what I accomplished? What kind of standards do I hold myself to? Once I have succeeded will I want to establish new goals?

Feedback

Feedback should be immediate, objective, specific, and directly related to your goals and targets. It should be simple and understandable, given on a regular basis. Effective feedback is also descriptive rather than evaluative, never mean-spirited, critical, or sarcastic. Feedback is a helpful way of giving and receiving help, especially if you want to learn how to match your behavior with your intentions.

1. Give yourself feedback by considering some or all of the following.
    a. Review what you did this week.
    b. How does it compare with your previous week?
    c. Set three priorities for next week.
    d. Will you want help with what you want to achieve?
    e. If you'd like assistance or advice, how might you ask for it in a way that a busy person will want to help you? Later, how will you say thanks?
    f. Think about ways to improve your behavior, thinking, habits and favorite hobbies or sport activities.
    g. What have you read or observed recently that has made an impact?
    h. What have been your recent accomplishments?
    i. What progress have you made in your habits, skills and relationships?
    j. Write next week's action plan.

2. Give it your all. Choose a realistic goal, monitor it closely, evaluate how you are doing, and make adjustments.

Marty is a good manager in an organization in northern California. In a performance review he was told by business colleagues that they did not perceive him to be a good listener. His wife, Janet, agreed with that assessment. Marty asked for help and set up a SMART goal plan. He started by asking himself why he did not listen carefully to others. He wrote the following:

I hear very little because I'm thinking about what I think the other person is really thinking or feeling.

I am thinking about what I am going to say next.

I change the topic very quickly and focus on myself.

It's like I have a filter in my brain: I hear only what I want to hear.

I hear what the other person said, but I quickly discount it.

I start to think about something else. I get bored easily.

Marty's SMART goals:

Specific: Improve my listening skills first with my wife, Janet.

Measurable: I will ask Janet after each time we interact, "On a scale from 1 to 5—1 is poor, 5 is great—what is your perception of me as a listener?" I will carry a piece of paper and mark down Janet's rating. Is it different from the rating I gave myself? If so, why? Gather some ratings during the first week to serve as a baseline. Am I the same Monday through Friday as I am on the weekend?

Attainable: I was averaging a 2 from her feedback during the first week, so I set a goal to get to be a 4 within a month's time.

Relevant: This is an important skill that will improve our marriage, especially as our children reach their teenage years and we need to work together as parents.

Time-bound: Set weekly improvement targets; see overall improvement within one month.

By measuring Janet's perceptions Marty realized that altering a few key behaviors, such as increasing eye contact, staying on the topic, and asking relevant questions, made a major difference in his wife's perception of his listening. Within two weeks he rated between a 3 and 4 on his personal measurement chart, up from his starting point of 2. And by listening to her, he demonstrated to her how important she is to him.

Marty also developed his listening skills by asking his colleagues and friends to give him honest feedback. He told his closest friends what he was doing with Janet and asked them to remind him if he seemed not to be listening to her or to them. That step showed Janet how important the goal had become to Marty. "I'm still working on this," Marty says. "Sometimes I slip, but there is no question that my relationship with Janet, my friends, and colleagues have significantly improved."

My SMART goal

Specific:

Measurable:

Attainable:

Relevant:

Time-bound:

What resources must I allocate?

How much time must I give to this goal?

Will there need to be changes in my schedule?

Who can help me?

Action

What will I do in the next 6 to 12 months?

What will I do in the next 1 to 5 years?

What have others done to achieve this goal?

What resistance must be minimized for this goal to be achieved?

Measures of success

How will I measure my success with regard to this goal?

How will I celebrate my progress toward my goal?

Who are my allies and how can they help?

EXERCISE 10

Mentors

Continually developing people share something in common—they are involved in mentoring relationships. If you look back on your past, you will recall people who have been your mentors. Now might be a good time to take out your photo or school albums and think about people who have in some way influenced who you are today. Write the names of people you believe have helped shape your life and how they've helped you.

To whom might you be a mentor in the future? How?

Upward Mentors

People who have helped you to become who you are—a grandparent, parent, coach, author, or someone you have never met personally

Friendship Mentors

People with whom you have experienced the stages of life—college, career, family, etc.

Sandpaper Mentors

People who have rubbed you the wrong way in life but have helped sharpen you

Downward Mentors

People you have invested in

Having reflected on the relationships that were important in shaping who you are today, now think about the people who can help you shape the life you desire. Write the names of people you believe are important to your personal and career development.

For each person you have mentioned above, write the type of mentor he or she is to you and the role each might play in helping you in implementing your goals.

Why is this person a good and reliable mentor? How long have I known this person or persons? Do I trust him or her as my ally?

How can this person or persons assist or advise me in realizing my desired future?

How can I use what I have learned to help others as others have helped me?

Choose two people from your mentor list and write them a letter sharing with them the ways they have helped shape your life.

EXERCISE 11

Consider the good things happening in your life right now. Write your thoughts in your journal, using the following questions to help prompt your reflection.

What do you enjoy most about the life you have created so far? How do you continue or duplicate those kinds of experiences? Who are your loved ones? How do you reciprocate what they do for you?

How do they know you appreciate them? What attention do you offer them in terms of time, consideration, and enjoyment? Are you early or on time for your appointments with them? Do you give them your undivided attention? Do you really listen to them or are you thinking about what you are going to say before they finish? Do you look into their eyes when you speak with them? A friend's daughter once told us, "If you don't look someone in the eyes when you talk to them, the conversation doesn't count."

After your personal retreat has ended, how will you make your interactions with everyone you encounter more significant, pleasant, and enjoyable?

EXERCISE 12

Memories made and memories in the making

Look at the most recent photographs you brought with you. What feelings come up as you look at them: gratitude, appreciation, comfort, or something else? Write those feelings or reactions on a separate page or in a journal.

Think about ways you will create new, positive experiences in the year ahead— experiences that, when you review them during future retreats, you will remember with strong, positive feelings. Describe those experiences. Where are you? What are you doing? Who is with you?

As one of your action steps toward achieving your personal success plan, set a date on your calendar to revisit the work you have done on your personal retreat (preferably one year from now).

Month _____ Day _____ Year _____

Your personal retreat is almost complete. One last thing: Take another picture of yourself. How does it compare with the picture you took before your retreat started? Write your answer and refer to it often in the months to come. If someone you love and who loves you looked at the picture, how might he or she describe you?

The End of Your Retreat and the Beginning of a Better Life

Many of the people we have worked with say that keeping a journal of their progress for the first three months of their journey was a small discipline that made the significant changes in their life more permanent and maintainable. Often it resulted in keeping a journal on a permanent basis because of the positive results. Those who do take the time to journal say that getting up 30 minutes earlier than usual is all that's needed. Start by getting up 5 minutes earlier, then 10, 15, until after six weeks you wake up 30 minutes earlier without an alarm clock. Don't be surprised if after a few months that you are getting up an hour earlier and you are exercising and going for a walk as well. When you begin your day feeling that you start your day instead of having it start you, you will maintain that confident feeling for a longer and longer period of time until it lasts all day. What does the result of doing that look like? It looks like you are confident, engaged, personable, thoughtful, truthful, kind, and loving your life!

Have you found that the things that most concerned you or that you were afraid to come to grips with in the past seem lessened or gone? If not, you may want to refer to some of the earlier chapters in the book and review. In the worst-case scenario, even if you haven't decided today precisely what you will do to make improvements in your life, undoubtedly you are now keenly aware of what those changes need to and will be. In time the appropriate options, choices, and decisions will become eminently clear to you by asking yourself the following questions that define your Four-Dimensional Thinking:

Who are you and what do you want? What are the cores of your personal strengths, passions, and aspirations? How will you erase the imagination gridlock that has kept you from going after your authentic goals?

Where are you and why are you there? With this retreat acting as your compass, you are now creating your own life map because you better understand how you have arrived where you are right now. You have just reviewed your past choices and decisions and recognize your faulty thought and belief systems that somehow went undetected. And now you know good choices and decisions that bear repeating.

What will you do and how will you do it? It's great to dream, but as we said earlier, whenever your dreams collide with reality, reality always wins. Now you have a new direction to ensure a more successful, enjoyable life journey. You may not know exactly where you are going from point A to B, but you now know where you're not going anymore! In the months to come, you will become more and more calm and relaxed about what you will do and how you will do it because through reading this book and taking this retreat, the natural reaction is always more confidence in yourself and in what you are doing.

Who are your allies and how can they help? Your stable relationships are key in accomplishing your life goals. Your relationships with your family, loved ones, friends, and coworkers will never be the same. You now know how to better preserve and protect those relationships, and you will get even better with time. Flying solo isn't fun or safe for long stretches of time, and you will never lack for friends or allies because now you are a better and trusted friend and ally as well. You know how to think Four-Dimensionally, and your life has already changed for the better.

Congratulations on completing your own *Who Am I and What Do I Want?* Personal Retreat! You have made the decision to take control of the only life you already have total control over. As this chapter ends you are about to enter a new chapter in your life. Go home safely and happily, go to work with renewed vigor giving it your all, be with people you love, have fun, and plan to mentor others to do the same!

Stay true to your path. You are embarking on the journey for the best of your life for the rest of your life!

Notes

Chapter 1

1. Michael J. Silverstein and Neil Fiske, *Trading Up: Why Consumers Want Luxury Goods... And How Companies Create Them* (New York, Portfolio Penguin Group USA, 2003).

2. Gregg Easterbrook, *The Progress Paradox* (New York, Random House, 2004). "The Search for Meaning," *Trends Magazine* July 2004.
http://www.trends-magazine.com/trend.php/Trend/1009/Category/56

3. J. Gosling and H. Mintzberg, "Five Minds of a Manager," *Harvard Business Review* (November 2003).

Chapter 3

1. George Reavis, The Animal School, (Peterborough, NH, Crystal Springs Books, 1999).

Chapter 4

1. Daniel Goleman, Richard Boyatzis, and Annie McKee, *Primal Leadership: Realizing the Power of Emotional Intelligence* (Boston: Harvard Business School Press, 2002).

2. Center for Creative Leadership
http://www.ccl.org/leadership/pdf/news/newsletters/acrosstheboard.pdf
http://www.ccl.org/leadership/update/2004/AUGtransition.aspx?pageId=966

Chapter 5

1. Kurt Lewin, Defining the "Field at a Given Time." *Psychological Review*. 50 (1943): 292–310.

2. J.C. Norcross, A.C. Ratzin, and D. Payne, "Ringing in the New Year: The Change Processes and Reported Outcomes of Resolutions," *Addictive Behaviors* 14 (1989): 205–212.

Chapter 6

1. J. Robert Clinton and Paul D. Stanley, *Connecting: The Mentoring Relationships You Need to Succeed in Life* (Colorado Springs: NavPress, 1992).

2. Tom Rath, *Vital Friends: The People You Can't Afford to Live Without* (New York: Gallup Press, 2006).

3. J. Luft and H. Ingham, "The Johari window, a graphic model of interpersonal awareness," *Proceedings of the western training laboratory in group development.* (Los Angeles: UCLA. 1955).

Chapter 7

1. Laura Nash and Howard Stevenson, Just Enough: Tools for Creating Success in Your Work and Life (Hoboken, NJ: John Wiley and Sons, 2004).

Appreciation and Praise

We would like to thank our agent and partner, Margret McBride, for her extraordinary support in *Who Are You and What Do You Want?* She really made it happen. Her passion, talent, and involvement at every level helped make it fun and exciting; and she added the quality that makes this book something we are all very proud of. Margret brought out the best in all of us in thinking and writing, and in gathering the real-life examples that make this work come to life. We also want to thank her tireless team of Faye Atchison, Donna DeGutis, and Anne Bomke, who gave their all and were always there for us. Thank you, McBride Literary Agency. We will forever be grateful.

Thanks to:

Ken Blanchard for his continued support, friendship, and inspiration throughout our lives

Ken Sidey, editor at Meredith Books, for the great job of editing and staying on top of the never-ending details.

Chip Espinoza for his ideas and insights on the personal retreat.

Karla Jeffries, Senior Vice President; Doug Guendel, Vice President and General Manager; Amy Nichols, Director, Marketing and Publicity; Mark Mooberry, Marketing Product Manager; Greg Kayko, Editor in Chief; Chad Jewell, Associate Design Dirctor; Larry Erickson, Editor at Large; Jane Merten, Associate Product Manager; and all the Meredith Books publishing and sales team for believing in the message in this book.

Jim Dowd and his agency for making sure the right people get this life-changing message.

The many people who read the manuscript and gave us feedback.

All the talented people who gave us real-life examples of the principles in this book: Trudy Atchison, Tony Batts, Rolf Benirschke, Chuck Boppell, Lynne Cage, Dale Carlsen, Cholene Espinoza, Antwone Fisher, Pat Gillick, Steve Hadley, Vicki Halsey, Fred Haise, Frances Hesselbein, Mary Hunt, James Kennedy, Catherine Kinney, Peter Klein, Patrick Lencioni, Jane Roeder, Rachael Schreiber, Mike Scioscia, David Shakarian, Melanie Washington, Jonathan W., and Mike Ziegler.

The professors, researchers, and teachers who taught us about the many models for life planning.

John Wooden for his personal support and for being an inspirational model for *Who Are You and What Do You Want?*

The students, businesspeople, associates, and friends who individually and in groups have gone through our life-planning process and retreats.

Our fabulous "kids": Mark and Michelle; and Tracie, Lindie, and Kaylie. We love you!

Authors' Bios

Mick Ukleja is the founder and president of LeadershipTraQ, a leadership-consulting firm based in California. He hosts *Leadership-TraQ Televised*, an interview-format talk show in Southern California that profiles outstanding leaders. He helped found the Ukleja Center for Ethical Leadership at California State University, Long Beach, the second largest university in the state. He has worked with entrepreneurs and corporate executives of businesses and organizations ranging from Boeing to the Special Olympics. Mick also serves as Chairman of the Board of Trustees for the Astronauts Memorial Foundation at the Kennedy Space Center, which oversees the Center for Space Education. He is a principal in The Bonita Bay Group, one of the largest developers of master-planned communities in Southwest Florida. Dr. Ukleja holds a bachelor's degree in philosophy, a master's degree in Semitic languages, and a Ph.D. in theology.

Robert Lorber is president of the Lorber Kamai Consulting Group formed in Orange County, California. The organization has developed and implemented productivity improvement systems for companies on five continents. Its client roster includes Kraft Foods, Teichert Inc., Occidental Petroleum, Gillette, American Express, Mattel, AlliedSignal, Raley's, VSP, Wells Fargo, Pillsbury, Pfizer, and many other medium-size and Fortune 500 companies. Robert is an internationally recognized expert and published author on executive coaching, performance management, teamwork, and strategy development. He is the coauthor with Ken Blanchard of the *New York Times* and international best seller *Putting the One Minute Manager to Work*. He co-authored *Safety 24/7* with Gregory Anderson and *Doing What Matters* by Jim Kilts, former CEO of Gillette, and John Manfredi. Dr. Lorber received a master's degree in sociology and a Ph.D. in organizational psychology.

Services and Resources

Mick frequently keynotes on the subjects of Managing the Next Generation, Teamwork, Transformational Leadership, The Power of Empowerment, Ethical Leadership, and many more.

To learn more about Mick and LeadershpTraQ please visit
leadershiptraq.com
genextconsulting.com
ucel.org

Services and Resources

Bob Lorber is a personal coach for CEOs and business leaders throughout the world. He is a highly regarded management consultant who works with executive teams to improve their leadership skills, personal effectiveness, and the overall performance of their companies.

Bob offers consulting services, executive coaching, and executive retreats. He does keynote speeches on the subjects of Leadership and Change, Doing What Matters, Productivity Improvement, Team Development and Personal Life Planning, and Who Are You and What Do You Want? Bob and his organization help to align learning and improvement needs with business and individual strategies for long-term impact.

To learn more visit:
Lorber Kamai Consulting
lorberkamai.com
levylorber.com

What people are saying about
Who Are You and What Do You Want?

"This book will help you discover some special things about yourself. Life is short—get going with all the hopes and dreams you've accumulated! This book helped me and will help you with the journey called LIFE."

Ruthie Bolton, Sacramento Monarchs all-star basketball player and two-time Olympic gold medal winner

"Three words: Read this book! It contains the wisdom and the power to turn your life around and drive you to success. Solid, practical, and brilliant, *Who Are You and What Do You Want?* is a book I'm buying for all my grown children and begging them to read and apply. Bob Lorber and Mick Ukleja have created what I predict will become an instant classic."

Sheldon Bowles, best-selling author of *Raving Fans* and *Gung Ho*

"What a refreshing, profound, and practical book! Mick Ukleja and Robert Lorber have given us a gift. It's a gift of understanding and wisdom. Read this book! It could change your life."

Steve Brown, professor, Reformed Seminary; author and teacher on the syndicated program *Key Life*

"The book is divine. In a simple-to-understand yet confident tone, it explains that setting goals, putting them on paper, and living the truth will help you achieve all that is truly 'you.'"

Stuart Brownstein, partner, Colin Cowie Lifestyle

"I had rationalized my lifestyle and defined it as 'balance.' This penetrating book has blown my sculptured definition out of the water and challenged me to take back my life for what is truly important."

Steven K. Buster, husband; president and CEO of The Mechanics Bank

"*Who Are You and What Do You Want?* is a marvelous personal planning tool. With its practical and detailed approach, it has helped me bring clarity to my own life journey and will undoubtedly help many others do the same. This is the one we will use."

Bill Coyne, CEO and president, Raley's

"A wonderful journey guide for living a fully engaged life."

John Christensen, CEO ChartHouse Learning, creator of the FISH! philosophy, and co-author of FISH! books

"It seems as though we leaders are busier and more dissatisfied than ever. Success is not leading to satisfaction. Thankfully this great book has come along to offer refreshing hope of a more balanced and sustainable life through Four-Dimensional Thinking. I recommend this book highly to every overextended leader battling commitments and the clock. It is filled with practical wisdom that points us to a better place, what the authors call a realistic and satisfying life map."

Dr. Hans Finzel, president and CEO of WorldVenture, author of the best seller *The Top Ten Mistakes Leaders Make*

"Ukleja and Lorber have created a must read (and follow!) road map for those who wish to make significant, positive changes in the direction of their lives."

Ned Guillet, former senior vice president-human resources, The Gillette Company

"What a refreshing, motivating read! What you hold in your hands does what most leadership books fail to do—it asks the right questions, follows with the right answers, plus gives a blueprint for how to change and achieve success for the rest and the best of your life. I like that, and so will you!"

Mary Hunt, founder DebtProofLiving.com, speaker, best-selling author of *Live Your Life for Half the Price*

"So often we make life-affecting plans based on where we think we are rather than where we really are. Read this book. For all ages it brings us back to reality and blueprints the path to the life each of us longs for."

Ethan Jackson, chairman, CEO, Basic American Financial, Inc.

"This is an excellent book for anyone wanting self-improvement or, as the authors say, "self-leadership." The personal testimonies came alive and leaped off the pages for me. I was particularly touched by the reminder to do those things I do well and leave the other 80 percent (or more) to someone who does them better."

William S. Kanaga, retired chairman, Ernst & Young; former chairman, U.S. Chamber of Commerce

"This short and readable book is packed full of lessons for anyone interested in living a more purposeful life. Whether you're graduating from college, planning your retirement, or living somewhere in between, *Who Are You* should not only be read but kept next to the nightstand for regular review and reminder."

Patrick Lencioni, president, The Table Group; best-selling author of *The Five Dysfunctions of a Team*

"A great resource for self-discovery, this book prods you in all the right places to help you achieve the best of your life."

Carl H. Lindner III, co-CEO, American Financial Group

"You can't learn a more valuable lesson than the one taught in this book: Truth and honesty with yourself and others is essential to a successful life. That principle plus the techniques and exercises in this book are a recipe for greater meaning and accomplishment in your life."

David Lucas, chairman, The Bonita Bay Group

"*Who You Are and What Do You Want?* provides an excellent road map toward clarifying and achieving your career and life goals. Through a series of real-life examples and exercises, the authors facilitate the process of self-discovery necessary for success and fulfillment in all aspects of one's life. Get this book—it's all you'll need."

Rob Lynch, president and CEO of VSP

"Are you getting exactly what you want out of life? Most of us aren't, but we don't know what to do about it. Mick Ukleja and Bob Lorber will get you started on a new path, and their Four-Dimensional Thinking will give you a fresh perspective on your life, your goals, and your ultimate happiness."

Kathy Matthews, coauthor of *The Wall Street Diet, SuperFoodsRx,* and other best sellers

"This is a must-read for anyone who wants to get serious about life and to achieve the results he or she has often dreamed of."

Patrick McClenahan, senior vice president, CBS-2 and KCAL-9 Television

"I implore you to embark on a journey for 'the best of your life.' Mick and Robert provide the insights and tools necessary to identify signs in everyday life that act as a road map to a rewarding future. I highly recommend this book as a personal and professional instrument for success."

Robert McKnight, founder and CEO of Quicksilver, Inc.

"This easy read takes goal-setting and strategic-planning theories and boils them down to simple, straightforward steps presented in layman's language. Following these steps will increase your efficiency, provide clarity to your life, and provide peace of mind, knowing you're not running in sand."

Ron Mittelstaedt, president and CEO, Waste Connections, Inc.

"The greatest feeling in life is knowing who you are, doing what you love, and living the life you enjoy. This book leads you to that place if you aren't there already—and if you are, it helps you appreciate your accomplishments! This is a great way to HUG yourself and those you care about. The 48-hour personal retreat is something everyone wants to take!"

Jack Mitchell, CEO, Mitchells/Richards/Marshs; author of *Hug Your Customers* and *Hug Your People*

"I found *Who Are You and What Do You Want?* genuinely useful in helping me gain personal insight and think meaningfully about my future."

Jud Riggs, CEO, Teichert Inc.

"In any bookstore business section, there are more words than wisdom. Most treatises focus on the enterprise, but the real challenge begins with the individuals. Ukleja and Lorber know that without maximized people, you can never maximize the organization. Listen to their insights; benefit from their perspectives. They expose the catalysts for real and lasting leverage."

Bob Shank, founder/CEO, The Master's Program

"Many of us need a road map to a life of meaning. This provides that map and the guideposts along the way!"

Lynn Schenk, former congresswoman from California and former chief of staff to the Governor of California

"This book is an inspiration to anyone who wants to understand and embrace all aspects of their life, giving them the courage to make lasting changes by utilizing their own unique gifts and passions."

Bill Shumard, president and CEO, Special Olympics Southern California

"The principles in this book relate directly to my career and my goal to play the best tennis of my life. Like the message, I needed to reflect, be honest with myself, plan a course of action, and get some help to get it done. This book is great for all ages and stages of life and has had a much broader application for my life—beyond my short tennis career."

Stan Smith, Wimbledon and U.S. Open champion
and former No. 1-ranked player in the world

"This book asks the questions that will help you grow. The authors are not just talking heads; they come from the experience of 'been there, done that.' Their book opens the oyster shell to find the pearl in you. A must-read for your growth."

Jim Tunney, Ed.D., former NFL referee, educator,
and author of *It's the Will, Not the Skill*

"As more and more of us are hitting 'the pause button' to reflect on who we are, where we are going, and what we will do with the rest of our lives, this book offers a coherent framework and useful tools for what the authors describe as a 'personal global positioning process.' It is full of provocative questions and nuggets of wisdom that will help the reader rebalance, realign, and reenergize his or her life."

Mary Lindenstein Walshok, sociologist and Dean of
Extension at the University of California San Diego

"*Who Are You and What Do You Want?* takes you on a great journey toward meaningful self-actualization. From the thought-provoking stories to the personal retreat exercises, this book is a blueprint for all of us to follow."

Michael Ziegler, president and CEO, PRIDE Industries

Notes and follow-up review

Notes and follow-up review

Notes and follow-up review

Notes and follow-up review

Notes and follow-up review